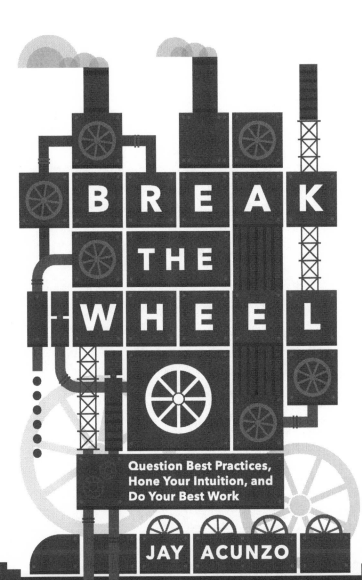

BREAK THE WHEEL

Question Best Practices, Hone Your Intuition, and Do Your Best Work

JAY ACUNZO

BREAK THE WHEEL

Question Best Practices, Hone Your
Intuition, and Do Your Best Work

ISBN   978-1-5445-0105-5 *Paperback*

        978-1-5445-0104-8 *Ebook*

        978-1-5445-0106-2 *Audiobook*

For Xandra—you inspire me to do what's best and be my best, every single day. I love you.

For my daughter, whose name is still a surprise at the time of this writing—may you live your life based on what's best for you and you alone, regardless of the conventional path. As I write these words, I'm still a few months from meeting you, but I already love you. Like, a ton.

CONTENTS

PRAISE. KIND OF.

ACTUAL THOUGHTS FROM JAY ACUNZO'S ACTUAL READERS, NOT EXPERTS DOING HIM A FAVOR.

In 1855, after reading Walt Whitman's Leaves of Grass, Ralph Waldo Emerson sent the young poet a congratulatory letter. "I greet you at the beginning of a great career," he wrote. The following year, when Whitman published a second edition of the same collection, he printed those words in gold leaf along the spine, and thus, "blurbs" were born.

Blurbs are the promotional quotes that authors put on their books (and websites, and social media, and neck tattoos...you get it). There's nothing wrong with them, per se. They've just become a bit gnarled over the years. Rather than unsolicited words of encouragement, they're manufactured requests for praise—favors called in from one author to others. Whether or not the others have spent meaningful time with the text is unclear.

Today's blurbs are badges more similar to pieces of flair worn by a waiter at Chili's than proud symbols of achievement on a boy or girl scout's sash—symbols that are hard-won through hard work.

For reasons you'll soon learn in this book, Jay Acunzo broke from the convention and asked his email subscribers to blurb his writing. These are actual comments from actual, longtime readers.

✳ ✳ ✳

"Acunzo's writing and storytelling are unmatched in the generally droll B2B space. He finds unique ways to inspire, enlighten, and reinvigorate an audience who can be easily burnt out and underappreciated in their creative tasks. Jay has created a tribe and a community around daring to be great and defying best practices in a world that thrives on mediocrity."

—AMBER VAN MOESSNER, DIRECTOR OF
CONTENT MARKETING, NEW YORK, NY

"I love Jay's enthusiastic style, his big ideas, and his willingness to challenge and change the world. He's not afraid to say what

others won't in a way others can't. No one tells a story like Jay, and the lessons...OH...the lessons."

—ANDREW DAVIS, AUTHOR AND KEYNOTE SPEAKER, BOCA RATON, FL

"It sounds so cheesy to say, but Jay's words light my soul on fire and just make me want to do amazing things. His writing is a manifesto for rediscovering and unleashing passion and pride for the work we're all doing."

—MELISSA STEVENS, DIRECTOR OF DIGITAL MARKETING, BOSTON, MA

"When I read anything from Jay, it feels like he's talking directly to me. Every. Single. Time. His honesty is contagious and a reflection of his understanding of people. It's baffling, like some sort of sorcery."

—HALEY NEID, BRAND MANAGER, DALLAS, TX

"Jay is seemingly able to convert my sentiments into words that I can forward to my teams. He is an idealist in the best possible way. He says the things that many are thinking but are afraid to say for fear of disregarding the prevailing best practices."

—STEVE RADICK, VP OF PR, PITTSBURGH, PA

"I love that Jay demands to know, Is this the right way, or is it just the way we're all traveling because...we're all traveling that way? Few people offer truly original, deeply

PRAISE. KIND OF. · 11

thoughtful, and highly useful contributions. Jay does. Every time."

—SHERENE STRAHAN, UNIVERSITY MARKETING
MANAGER, PERTH, AUSTRALIA

"Jay's unabashed glee for the process of creation comes through in everything he writes. His writing style evokes an honest and sincere conversation between friends. Anyone who likes to create in any capacity will appreciate Jay's work."

—ADAM P. NEWTON, SENIOR CONTENT
STRATEGIST, HOUSTON, TX

"Jay's writing is conversational, approachable, and relatable in a way that lots of business writing isn't. I can always count on him for a 'straight shooter' approach, sharing the things that others may not be willing or able to say about our industry."

—MELANIE DEZIEL, ENTREPRENEUR AND
CONSULTANT, NEW YORK, NY

"Jay sees the people, not the practice, which equates to pushing for better versions of ourselves rather than better versions of marketing."

—ANTHONY COPPEDGE, AGILE MARKETING
CONSULTANT, OKLAHOMA CITY, OK

"It's refreshing to read something so relevant and down to earth. Jay is relatable for readers like me who feel as though

they're working out at least five different things every time they sit down to work."

—CARLA ALDERSON, SERVICE OPERATIONS
MANAGER, HALIFAX, NOVA SCOTIA

"Every story feels personal, like we're sitting around catching up over a beer. Jay has a unique voice and take that will get you thinking about your own work and life in ways you probably haven't considered before."

—CHRIS COOPER, ENTREPRENEUR
AND WRITER, DENVER, CO

"In a world where everyone is suddenly an expert, Jay isn't trying to add himself to any lists. He breaks through the BS and helps unlock new ways to think about creative work. If you're feeling stuck or uninspired or jaded, Jay's writing will pull you out of your funk and get you excited about what you can do."

—LEE PRICE, MANAGING EDITOR, VALDOSTA, GA

"Jay's way of spotlighting stories and creators will end up inspiring you to jump the unthinkable gaps you've set up in your mind."

—BEN H. ROME, MARKETING CREATIVE, WASHINGTON, DC

"If you're tired of emotional pablum and lifeless marketing, give Acunzo a look. He's not afraid to take a very different stance than the 'others.'"

—STAN DUBIN, PRESIDENT AND CONSULTANT, CLEARWATER, FL

"Instead of reading regurgitated ideas on a boring business blog, read this instead. Everyone preaches authenticity and creativity, but this guy actually practices it day in and day out."

—BEN SAILER, BLOG MANAGER, FARGO, ND

"Jay's work is for people who hate self-help formulas. His work is a display of case studies and creative challenges meant to spark your own genius."

—HEATHER DOLLAR, DESIGNER, RALEIGH, NC

CHAPTER 1

THE WHEEL

"The day of reckoning is upon us, my brothers! What is life, if not to die a glorious death?"

The Viking leader stood at the back of his ship, barking at his men as a storm threatened to overturn them.

"Fear not, for tonight we drink in the halls of Valhalla! Row! Awaken, and welcome death!"

Seconds later, their ship tumbled over a waterfall... straight into a man's mouth. Millions of people laughed.

Those people were watching the Super Bowl, and those Vikings were part of a commercial for Death Wish Coffee. Television airtime during the big game carries a hefty price tag—upwards of $5 million per thirty seconds—but Death Wish ran this ad for free.

For the average small business, a free Viking-themed Super Bowl ad would be the most surprising thing about them, but if we were coffee experts, we might point to something else. If we were coffee experts, we might be surprised to learn Death Wish is able to survive at all, let alone thrive as it is today. In fact, if we were coffee experts, an early decision made by the company's founder might seem so unconventional, we'd consider it unthinkable.

And here's the thing: It *is* unthinkable. Until you hear his side of the story.

Death Wish founder and CEO Mike Brown mostly wears black hoodies, jeans, and work boots. He has short brown hair and a close-cropped beard—both touched with gray—and a broad, warm smile. Although he loves the work he does at Death Wish, he didn't set out to start this company. He didn't set out to work in the coffee industry whatsoever.

His journey began in Saratoga Springs, New York. It's one of those classically northeastern American towns. Squat, brick buildings with local shops and restaurants dot the main street, and plenty of leafy green neighborhoods weave all around it. Lots of blue-collar workers call the area home, while lots of New York City residents, living 200 miles south of Saratoga, call it "that place with the horse racing."

In 2008, Mike Brown felt like his career had stumbled out of the gate. He'd earned a master's degree in accounting because he figured that's what a successful professional does. But after landing a job following graduation, he realized he hated accounting. He was miserable, so he quit.

After a few weeks of lounging around local coffee shops without any prospects or ideas, Mike decided to start a coffee shop of his own. He called it Saratoga Coffee Traders.

As you've probably experienced firsthand, most coffee shops look the same. Sure, there are a few incremental differences: a pristine white display case, a new twist on a familiar drink, and, wait a second, is that some extra exposed brick I see? (My millennial senses are tingling!) But for the most part, every coffee shop experience feels identical. Mike knew this all too well. After spending countless hours in those establishments, growing increasingly frustrated with the commodity feel, he decided to build something different.

Unfortunately, simply *aspiring* to create something exceptional doesn't guarantee you will. You still need to make the right decisions to succeed, and despite Mike's admirable intentions, he was making some terrible decisions. For instance, to liven up his menu, he decided to sell twenty-five different blends of coffee. Even worse, he carried more than two hundred different types of candy. (Yes! At a coffee shop!) So in one sense, I guess Mike succeeded in building a different kind of experience than the average coffee shop. Of course, as he soon realized, it's not enough to simply be "different" than the average. Because Mike was tanking his business.

"I pretty much ran it into the ground," he said. He'd been open for less than a year, and he was already in danger of closing shop. "I actually painted out the worst-case scenario. If I lost everything—if I lost all my savings, and I had to sell my house and sell my car—what would be my worst-case scenario?"

He figured, God forbid, if all that happened, he'd move back in with his mother. He'd be damned if he'd return to accounting. He'd rather sell all of his belongings and move home.

"And that's *exactly* what happened," he said. "The exact worst-case scenario that could have happened, happened. It was even a little worse than that too. I had to borrow money from my mom to pay my employees."

To turn things around, Mike did what many of us would do in his shoes: he sought the advice of experts. Everyone he met, plus all the research he conducted, pointed to one fatal flaw in his business. Without realizing it, he had committed a mortal sin in the coffee industry. Mike was roasting the wrong type of coffee bean.

This realization, and Mike's subsequent reaction, would ultimately spawn the wildly successful Death Wish Coffee brand. But to understand what happened next and why it was so unthinkable to industry experts, we first need to know some basics about coffee beans.

The two most common types of coffee beans are called *arabica* and *robusta*. Arabica beans represent more than 70 percent of the world's coffee crop each year. That cute little cafe on the corner? They serve arabica. That bag of beans from the grocery store? Arabica. That grande-skinny-half-caff-Guatemalan-Casi-Cielo at Starbucks? Yeah, arabica.

This makes sense, since arabica is delicious. Robusta, on the other hand, can be borderline torture to drink. You typically encounter robusta beans in instant coffees, like those little sleeves of grounds you see in hotel rooms—the stuff you mix into hot water as you sob quietly over your mug. Robusta coffee is the kind of coffee that makes you weigh how badly you need your fix against how willing you are to have Nasty Old Man Breath for the next twenty-four hours.

In the minds of coffee experts, there is a right and a wrong bean to roast, and our friend Mike was roasting the wrong one. He came to the conclusion that if Saratoga Coffee Traders was going to succeed, he had to roast arabica beans. That's the best practice. That's what he should do.

One day, a customer walked into Mike's struggling shop and asked, "What's the strongest cup of coffee you can make?"

The customer was a truck driver about to embark on another long journey, so he told Mike he wanted something strong and dark. However, after all the research Mike had just done, he knew that "strong" and "dark" usually don't mix. (Despite what you might think, lighter coffees are more caffeinated.) So Mike did his best to satisfy his customer, pouring the truck driver the darkest roast he'd brewed that day, and the man went on his way.

As the shop fell quiet again, and Mike's anxiety about his business began to creep back into his mind, he realized he'd heard that request before, always from the same type of person: truck drivers, construction workers, and all these hard-charging, hardworking individuals. They would march into the shop and demand stronger *and* darker coffee. Mike wondered, "What if I surprised that group of people?" He set his sights on a new goal: Mike would create the world's strongest coffee.

That's a great aspiration, right? But more than merely

sounding good, this aspiration helped Mike make good decisions in a very concrete way. By stating his aspiration out loud, he turned that previously vague desire to do something great into something specific he could create. Before that moment, he'd tried everything and anything to figure out what "better than average" meant. Once he was able to articulate it, however, Mike regained a sense of clarity that he'd lost along the way.

Without realizing it, Mike had unhooked himself from the endless cycle that we each face whenever we make decisions at work. We'll explore this cycle in more detail later. For now, just know that it's the reason why so much commodity work exists today. This ubiquitous approach to making decisions is why so much work and so many careers plateau. Mike, on the other hand, eventually bridged the gap between commodity work and an exceptional career.

How can we do that too?

WHAT DOES YOUR "BEST WORK" EVEN MEAN?

Have you ever stopped to wonder what it really takes to do your best work? What does it take to do anything exceptional compared to the typical stuff shared around your industry?

A lot of ink and many more pixels have been used to

explore the traits of successful people. The idea here is that, if we can mimic them, we can be successful too. I'll admit, many of those books are well-intentioned and quite good to read. Unfortunately, most are crap on a cracker. Attempting to learn from others only goes so far. It's the same as simply relying on conventional thinking. All of this merely provides us with possibilities, not answers, and then it's up to us to vet those possibilities to ensure they'll work for us. That's what ultimately matters most, isn't it?

Unfortunately, vetting ideas or advice is not something most of us have been taught to do. It's not something we spend much time doing, either, especially when you consider how much time we put in learning from experts, looking for shortcuts, or even tinkering with the latest trends or tools. Rarely do we stop to wonder if we're making the best possible decisions for our specific situations. By the end of this book, that's what you'll be able to do. As we embark on this journey together, unlike most advice books, we're not looking to learn what it takes for "anyone" to do their best work. Instead, we'll focus on a much more important question: how can *you* start doing *yours*?

To figure that out, Mike Brown articulated his aspiration out loud to himself and to others: "I'll create the world's strongest coffee." With that statement in mind, he could begin to vet his ideas, as well as the endless advice of others, to make the best decision for his specific situation. Using that aspiration like a litmus test, he could more easily and confidently understand which idea or approach made sense, and to what degree. For example, when experts told Mike to stop selling twenty-five types of coffee and two-hundred types of candy, he instantly agreed. That advice made total sense for his situation. If you're going to create the world's strongest coffee, you can't be distracted with the cost, logistics, and marketing required to sell hundreds of products. On the other hand, when Mike was told to roast arabica beans instead of robusta, he confidently bucked the trend. Arguably, using arabica coffee was the most widely-accepted approach among coffee businesses in North America. Doing anything else would be foolish, almost crazy, but to Mike, roasting robusta beans seemed like the best decision for him. Why?

It turns out that roasted robusta beans contain more caffeine than roasted arabica beans. According to the Coffee Research Institute, one robusta bean is more than 2 percent caffeine, while one arabica bean is just over 1 percent. On average, a single cup of coffee made with robusta contains 83 percent more caffeine than the other stuff. If your aspiration is to create the world's strongest coffee, this information is pretty darn useful.

So, yes, *in general,* you should roast arabica beans for your coffee. But Mike isn't operating in a generality. He operates in a very specific situation, just like the rest of us. For Mike, it made more sense to reject the conventional approach and roast robusta coffee. As we know already, the last thing he wanted was to create another average coffee shop. However, only once he committed to creating the world's strongest coffee did Mike know what "better than the average" meant to him.

In our quest to do great work, Mike's aspirational statement holds a clue for how we might start our decision-making process. In later chapters, we'll explore the idea of aspirations in more detail and learn about a powerful heuristic called "aspirational anchors." For now, ask yourself: When you say you aspire to be exceptional instead of average, what exactly does that mean? In a world full of best practices, what are the *right* practices for you? What is your version of the robusta coffee bean?

Once Mike decided to roast robusta beans, he broke from experts in a stark way. But admittedly, conventional thinking still holds some value. It can tell us what worked in the past or what works for others, and when we need results, we'd be wise to consider that information. The whole "stand on the shoulders of giants" maxim feels valid, doesn't it?

So if you're Mike, and you're going to break from what

experts say to do, you better be damn sure that you're well-informed. In other words, it's not enough to merely break from conventional thinking. The goal is to understand our situation enough to know whether or not the conventional approach is right for us. When all Mike did was fight against the commodity coffee shop experience, he tanked his business. Not until he could explain why his way was better than the typical way did he actually see any results. If he started as a rebel without a cause, he then transformed into a rebel with a purpose—and that purpose was something coffee experts could never have anticipated.

Working behind the counter at Saratoga Coffee Traders that first year, Mike got to know who his customers were and what they wanted. His customers were truck drivers, construction workers, entrepreneurs, service workers and stable workers at racetracks, and other lace-up-your-boots and pick-up-your-pail types. Mike realized that these customers viewed coffee the same way they viewed Red Bull or Five Hour Energy: as a means to an end. Mike reasoned that if his customers wanted strong coffee, and they viewed coffee as a hasty transaction instead of a long, leisurely activity, then the chocolatey or fruity flavors promised by arabica roasts weren't as important. For Mike's customers, the goal was the outcome, not the experience. They wanted the ends, through whatever means necessary.

So what "ends" did Mike's customers want? In finding the answer, Mike was inspired by that simple question from that one truck driver. Remember, he wanted a dark and strong cup of coffee. What this man didn't realize, however, is that those two traits don't typically go together. You see, as all coffee experts know, darker roasts tend to be weaker. That's because the beans have been roasted for longer, removing more caffeine than in lighter roasts. But if Mike had shared this fact with the truck driver, in addition to losing that customer thanks to a rather condescending reply, he would have made two faulty assumptions that industry experts often make. First, in claiming that "strong" and "dark" don't typically go together, a coffee expert is assuming that the coffee in question is arabica. You can't create a dark roast that's also strong since, to get arabica coffee dark enough, you end up roasting away much of its caffeine. The second assumption is that the other common type of coffee, robusta, isn't a viable option, given the more bitter flavor and small inventory in North America. So now you have two choices: create a dark roast or a strong roast. You can't do both.

On average, these assumptions are true. But Mike isn't operating in an average situation. He didn't act like an expert, embracing what works in general. Instead, he acted like an investigator, looking for evidence of what could work in his specific situation, with his specific customers. His customers drank coffee like those chemical-flavored energy drinks. Robusta beans are fine. Darker and stronger coffee is possible. *I'll create the world's strongest coffee.* Mike's aspiration was both personal and logical. He wasn't a rebel without a cause at all.

Next, Mike extracted an insight from his data to ensure his aspiration matched what his customers were willing to buy. His data was simple, if qualitative: customers kept asking for strong coffee. Therefore, it's easy to make the assumption that customers *want* stronger coffee. But that's not a true insight—not yet. Instead, acting like a true investigator, Mike kept asking questions. *Why? Why do customers keep asking for stronger coffee? What is it about them in particular?*

Well, obviously, they want more caffeine. No?

Sure, Mike thought, *but why do they want more caffeine?*

Well, clearly, they want more energy during their day. Right?

Yes, but why do they want more energy during their day? What are they doing all day?

It's here that Mike found a useful insight—one that could challenge industry-wide assumptions of what works "in general" and help him tailor his decision-making. (When the answer to "Why?" stops feeling obvious, you know you're on the right track.) So, why did Mike's customers want more energy? *Well*, he thought, *they're truck drivers. They're construction workers. They're racetrack workers. They're hard-charging and—wait a second—*hardworking *individuals.*

Aha! There it is! These people don't want stronger coffee. They don't want more caffeine. They don't even want more energy. No, in reality, Mike Brown's customers want the ability to work themselves to death.

So that's exactly what he sells.

That's why the name "Death Wish Coffee" makes sense, although we laugh and shake our heads just hearing it. That's why Mike's aspiration is strategic, not fluffy or foolish or rebellious. That's why robusta beans are safe instead of risky. Mike had informed his aspiration with a fundamental insight about his customers. His customers work their butts off, and they reach for coffee for the end result, not the experience. They want the ability to work themselves to death, so that's what Mike should sell.

When we operate like Mike, like investigators, we stop acting like a commodity and become the exception. For instance, in the coffee business, plenty of brands sell strong coffee. Plenty of brands sell caffeine. Some brands even sell the idea of more energy during your day. But Mike and Death Wish Coffee are the only ones who sell the ability to work insanely hard. Had Mike copied the average approach, he'd have missed this opportunity. That's the danger of focusing on "what works" across a job function, company, or industry. We're at risk of relying on assumptions others are making about the specific details we face each day. "That works in general, so just follow that." What if we stopped relying on what works *in general?* After all, nobody operates in a generality.

Mike certainly didn't.

Mike operated in upstate New York—a detail that factored into his thinking and his decisions. To understand what I mean, consider the climate of Mike's home county, as well as the surrounding counties in New York state at the time.

According to a report by New York's Center for Economic Growth (CEG), the region's population was in rapid decline around the same time Mike was building his shop and, later, the Death Wish brand. Between April 1, 2010, and July 1, 2016, the population for upstate New York dropped by 93,530. When you factor in the death and birth rates, the region lost a total of 59,648 people over roughly six years. The reason was simple: jobs. Like many other areas in the United States, blue-collar jobs were getting outsourced or automated, while factories kept closing and laying off workers. Additionally, white-collar workers were relocating to major cities to follow the companies that could employ them. In the study, the CEG found that northern regions of New York were particularly hard hit.

Except for two.

Buried in the details of this report are two exceptions to the trend, two counties experiencing an influx of people instead of a decline: Albany and Saratoga. In fact, Saratoga county experienced a massive 3.4 percent population *increase* over the same period that other areas were losing residents—the largest such increase in the state. Thanks to the county's investments in technology, small business, and work-training initiatives, people poured into Saratoga Springs and the surrounding towns, and they all arrived for one reason: to work insanely hard.

That's what Mike's customers wanted, so that's what he sold. As a first step, his aspiration had turned his vague but burning desire to be exceptional into something specific and concrete. Next, his customer insight told him he could pursue that aspiration with confidence, informed by the specific situation in which he worked. Thus, Death Wish Coffee was born.

Take one look at the Death Wish brand today, and you'll notice just how much Mike's customer insight informs the entire company. Death Wish has a jet black and blood red color scheme with a white skull-and-crossbones icon. The brand identity clashes in menacing fashion with all the rustic browns, forest greens, or soft oranges used by the average coffee brands—brands that sell strong coffee or more caffeine, but not the ability to work yourself to death. (After all, America might run on Dunkin', but it sure as hell doesn't die on it.)

On Instagram, Death Wish shows off just how unique they are compared to their peers. Leather-clad employees lift huge, medieval-style clay mugs toward their even larger beards. Warehouse workers in faded denim uniforms glare at the camera, coffees in hand. Every few posts, the marketers at Death Wish share a motivational quote. While this is a pretty typical practice for a brand on social media, Death Wish manages to break from even this common convention. Instead of sunrises and mountain ranges and uplifting words from history's best thinkers, Death Wish shares quotes like, "It's a beautiful day to leave me alone," and, "I'd give up coffee, but I'd have to take up murder." My personal favorite reads, "Did you ever stop to think that maybe coffee is addicted to me?"

LET'S MAKE SHERLOCK PROUD

From their name and identity to the tiniest of details on social media, Death Wish is an exception in the coffee business, but they didn't arrive there by trying to be different from their peers. Instead, acting like an investigator led Mike to make decisions based on his own situation rather than the conventional wisdom of his space. Those details led him to something far different than the general thinking because he wasn't focused on generalities. Indeed, the difference between Death Wish and other coffee brands doesn't stop at the menacing logo or the aggressive anti-motivational quotes. The real, underlying reason Death Wish is exceptional is that they actually understand what makes them an exception.

When you and I act like investigators, we start to pay more attention to our audience than to the industry, and when that happens, the audience tends to pay more attention to us. We're so obsessed with industry echo chambers, which is a fine place to start, but remember what all of that information is for: your audience. It's all for the customer or reader or client or whomever you serve. What if we spent more of our time focused on them? In the end, experts may know what works in general, but investigators supplement that broad wisdom with evidence.

Admittedly, there's a balance. We constantly make decisions based on habit, precedent, or common knowledge.

Generalizing can feel inevitable or even quite helpful in making decisions. Can you imagine a world where every move was questioned without first conducting a rigorous investigation? We'd all be paralyzed. Still, the working world struggles to break free of conventional thinking even when companies or individuals know it's holding them back. The goal isn't to remove all generalizations but rather to establish a baseline understanding of our specific situation, each and every time we encounter a new one.

If Sherlock Holmes were real and, let's say, a digital marketer, he'd be a valuable asset to the team because he'd provide firsthand clues to supplement an industry flooded by secondhand advice. Just like this rather lame, thankfully fictional Sherlock, Mike Brown supplemented what he'd learned from studying his industry with firsthand knowledge of what he aspired to do and his customers yearned to buy. Achieving that kind of clarity required him to set aside conventional thinking for a moment in order to think for himself.

Ask yourself: Are you spending more time learning about your company or yourself? Do you spend more money getting up to speed on your industry or your customers?

Then, once we believe we know ourselves and our customers in theory, can we test our assumptions? That is exactly what Mike Brown did. He decided to test his aspiration and his customer insight by creating one batch of Death Wish Coffee. It was a simple, constrained project. He planned to create a single roast of Death Wish, with more caffeine than the average cup, to sell to one type of customer at some point that quarter at a rate of one bag per week. Those five details represented his constraints. If he succeeded within those limitations, he could expand, driven by the confidence that he was heading in the right direction. It's also worth noting that this new-and-improved Mike wasn't obsessed with yielding final results. Instead, he was looking for a sign that he was on the right path toward results. Little by little, he found it.

"We sold one bag a month, and then one bag a week," he said. "And then I remember bringing two bags per day to the post office, and I thought, 'This is the most amazing thing ever!' And pretty soon, I'd hired someone to help me out with social media and was thinking that this could be a real business someday."

With every step Mike took, he informed his decisions using his customers' reactions to his tests. Even though he dreamed of selling millions of bags of Death Wish Coffee, his first step was to sell one bag overall, then one bag per month, then one bag per week, and so on. Although the product's initial sales weren't huge, the initial customer reactions were.

On Twitter, one customer raved: "You haven't had coffee until you've had Death Wish!"

"Here we goooo!" tweeted another, with an image of the new Death Wish logo.

Mike hadn't sold a ton of Death Wish yet, but he'd witnessed a small number of people reacting in a big way to what he was doing. This wasn't the final success he craved, but it was a signal he was on the right path. So often in the business world, we overlook that strong signal. We seek final success or the big, topline number to justify our actions. When that doesn't come, we fall back on the conventional approach. Not Mike. He understands the signal inherent in emotional customer reactions. They're a sign you should keep going.

After seeing such strong responses from his early adopters, Mike expanded his tests. He found the right path. He could take all that pent-up passion and determination that previously caused him to sprint madly in all directions and focus it in the right direction, strategically, carefully, and confidently. So Mike created more bags of Death Wish. He hired that social manager, as well as a few warehouse workers to package and ship his product. He hired an agency to design the logo and build an initial website. He expanded his products to include seasonal flavors, Keurig cups, mugs, hats, shirts, and more. With every move he made, he looked for a passionate response from people as a sign he should invest more. If he didn't see it, he killed his tests. If he did, he leaned in harder. Step by step, Mike built a thriving e-commerce business out of the sputtering Saratoga Coffee Traders shop—a shop now on the rise thanks to its flagship product, billed to customers as "The World's Strongest Coffee." It's a global brand, shipping products all over the world. Actually, let me amend that statement—because it turns out Death Wish ships their products *out* of this world. On June 29, 2018, Death Wish sent their coffee into space.

Announced on their podcast, *Fueled by Death Cast*, the company partnered with SpaceX to send a specially made blend of freeze-dried Death Wish Coffee to the International Space Station. The process began a year prior, early in their podcast's run, when retired astronaut Nicole Stott appeared as a guest. On the show, she explained just how exhausted she felt after doing a "space walk" around the outside of the space station, in full gear, tethered to the side of the station's hull. After six and a half hours of physical and mental exertion, not to mention the extreme emotions Nicole recalls feeling seeing a stunning Earth stretching below her, all she wanted was a strong cup of coffee. *Death Cast* co-host Dustin Alexander, a.k.a. "The Amazing D-Man," then asked Nicole a simple question: "How do we get Death Wish Coffee into space?" As with most things the hosts say, it was meant as a joke.

"You know what?" Nicole mused. "Let's talk about that. I think people would love it."

A year later, thanks to Nicole's help and an assist from SpaceX, Death Wish Coffee was delivered to the International Space Station. "The World's Strongest Coffee" is now "The Galaxy's Strongest Coffee." (I guess Mike needs to update his aspiration.)

Mike Brown and Death Wish Coffee are generating exceptional results, not because Mike found a new trend or best practice to follow, but because he became the consummate investigator into his specific situation. He articulated his aspiration, found a customer insight, and then tested every decision with his customers.

Mike's work can teach us something powerful about building exceptional companies and careers: when we make learning the point, instead of the end results, we tend to get better end results.

Do you inform your decisions by investigating your situation or by finding what works in general? Have you given enough thought to what makes your context an exception from the norm, or do you rely on conventional thinking?

WHAT WE USUALLY TRY

This entire book is really about one principle: doing whatever works best for us. Although the differences between us and others may be small, I believe they make all the difference in the world. Informing your work using those details is the difference between doing something exceptional and being yet another average-something in your space.

The truth is, our world today is evolving faster than ever, so when someone claims to have "the" answer, the only thing we can say with certainty is that "the" answer will change. On the other hand, if we were to become masters of figuring things out in any given scenario, we'd be unstoppable. Rather than knowing what worked for the average person, we'd be equipped to constantly update our knowledge, inform our decisions, and customize our work to fit our own situation. What if we could always identify the best possible decision for us in our situation, regardless of how the situation changes?

To understand that, I believe your context holds the clues, not the conventional thinking, and with that information in hand, you can find more clarity and make better decisions. All that matters is that you do what works for you—even if, from the outside looking in, your work seems different, counter-cultural, or even crazy to others. Death Wish Coffee certainly looks radical compared to their peers.

Four years after Mike launched the company, the world watched as a Viking captain urged his men to keep rowing through the storm, only to tumble out of a mug and into the mouth of a disheveled-looking man. The man glances into his mug, satisfied. He smiles as a booming announcer cuts in: "Death Wish Coffee. Fiercely caffeinated."

On social media, Death Wish has over 700,000 passionate followers—people who see themselves reflected in the aggressive branding and who demand their coffee be both strong *and* dark. In 2015, those raving fans voted Death Wish to the top spot in a contest run by the tech company Intuit. Fifteen-thousand small businesses entered that contest, but Death Wish received the most votes. The grand prize? A free Super Bowl ad.

Thanks to the success of Death Wish, Mike no longer labors to keep a single coffee shop afloat. Instead, he runs a thriving global brand. He has an office, a team, and a place to live that isn't down the hall from his mother. Every year, Death Wish sells millions of dollars in products, while Mike has been featured everywhere from CNN to *The New York Times* to one very well-written and entertaining book that you were smart to buy. (Have I mentioned how good you look today?)

Through it all, despite the warnings of his peers and the musings of experts, despite his early thrashing and scuffling and trying each and every new idea that popped to mind, Mike never stopped thinking for himself.

"That's the thing about coffee," Mike later told me on my podcast, *Unthinkable*. "There are tons of people out there who are experts and think coffee should taste a distinct way, but you know, it's all a personal preference."

Mike aspired to do exceptional work. In his mind, the enemy wasn't failure; it was settling for average. As I've traveled the world as a keynote speaker and interviewed hundreds of creative people as a podcaster, I've met countless individuals who feel the same way as Mike. They're frustrated by average work and long to do something exceptional. Their stories seem crazy, until you hear their side of it. Then it seems rather logical and smart. What's the difference? That's what I want to learn in our journey together here.

In each one of my speeches for the past few years, I've asked the audience the same question: "On a scale of zero to ten, who here aspires to be a five?"

Crickets. Always. Except for that one smartass in the back with his hand up. (Dammit, Larry, I saw that!) But for the most part, it's dead silent in the room, and that's an obvious reaction to a pretty obvious question. Nobody aspires to be a five. But really think about why. Go ahead, I'll wait. (I literally can't move forward until your eyes do, so...)

Why doesn't anybody aspire to be a five out of ten?

Because five is average, right? And *nobody* aspires to be average. However, it's so easy for us to do average work. Just think about your own situation. Are you doing work you'd consider a ten out of ten all the time? Is your team? Your company? Your industry as a whole?

Why not? And if not, what are you doing instead?

Maybe you're doing work that feels repetitive. You just keep reusing something that worked in the past. Maybe you're copying others, trying anything and everything from companies or individuals who succeed. Maybe you're stuck, and you don't know how to move forward. Or maybe you're just not seeing the results you think you deserve, given how incredibly hard you're working. Whatever the case, too much of our work ends up feeling average. There's this gap that exists in our careers between the work we *aspire* to do and the work we're actually doing; between the results we *want* to see and the results we're actually seeing.

That's so damn frustrating! Isn't it? I just can't stop wondering why. Why does this gap exist? And more importantly, how do we close it or prevent it from existing in the first place?

So now we return to that troublesome question: what does it actually take to be exceptional?

If we examine our normal behavior when we typically try to close that gap, we'll find our answers. Because what do we normally do when we need better results?

We look for best practices.

THE 3 DANGEROUS WAYS WE FIND BEST PRACTICES

Our hope for best practices is that our work will look something like this chart.

We're doing our daily work, but then we encounter that gap between average and exceptional. We're not seeing the results or feeling as fulfilled as we want. Suddenly, we find a best practice and implement it, and we're whisked away to the promised land where finally we start doing our best work and seeing amazing results! That is our hope for best practices. But our reality looks a lot more like this one.

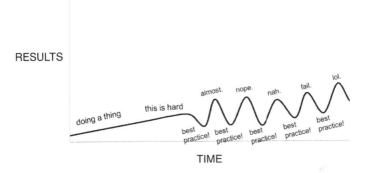

Over and over again, we find another best practice, and we just keep hoping and praying that one of them, one time, will finally deliver us better results. In the internet age, this process has gone insane. There's more information and advice out there than ever before. However, our problem isn't the volume of information; it's how we make sense of it all. Our biggest issue is how we make decisions in the workplace.

We tend to make our decisions in one of three ways, each of which can be rather troublesome.

Sometimes, we make decisions based on the best practice that carries the most weight in our minds. This is the path of conventional wisdom. The convention promises safety and certainty. It's the reliable approach, the tried-and-true. *Surely*, we think, *if it works for all of these people, it will work for me. Naturally,* we believe, *if the playbook worked back then, it will work for us now.*

But here's the problem: Just because something is the most common approach doesn't mean it's the *best* approach *for us.* Informing our decisions based purely on conventional wisdom only biases our thinking toward whatever the most people are saying or doing. That type of thinking doesn't guarantee we'll create exceptional work—not without knowing how or if it applies to us.

The newspaper industry learned this the hard way. In a column for *Fast Company,* bestselling author Shane Snow (*Smartcuts* and *Dream Teams*) shares the hilarious yet horrifying story that reveals the problem with conventional wisdom. Snow points to the decision made by *The Independent* in the early 2000s to reduce the size of the paper they used for their print editions. From the outside looking in, this decision seems unusual—until you understand their side of the story.

For centuries, newspapers were always printed on "broadsheets," large sheets of paper allowing for lengthy columns of text, typically measuring twenty-two inches tall. The first broadsheet newspaper was published in the Netherlands in 1618, but it didn't become the industry standard until nearly a century later. In 1712, the British government decided to tax newspapers based on the number of pages they used. In response, most publishers began using broadsheets. They'd found a loophole. They could publish just as many words and stories, but with fewer pages, thus avoiding steeper taxes.

That law was repealed in the 1800s, but by then, broadsheets had become the best practice. As a result, hundreds of years later, when *The Independent* decided to print on smaller pages, it seemed like a ridiculous decision. After all, everyone knows newspapers need to use twenty-two-inch pages! It'd be foolish to do anything different—except the decision to do something different worked better. According to the *Harvard Business Review*, the switch to more compact pages helped *The Independent* save money *and* generate more revenue.

I'd ask you: What's more foolish? Relying on a best practice established centuries ago, based on a law that no longer applies, or questioning that practice? In addition to being the product of a bygone era and obsolete tax, the main reason *The Independent* switched to compact pages didn't exist back when the best practice was first established: declining print revenue due to the internet.

Snow's article is appropriately titled "The Problem With Best Practices," and he cuts to the core of this ridiculousness when he writes, "The 'best practice' is one of the business world's most common conventions, but it's often arbitrary and based mainly on habit—the result of conditions that no longer apply."

Conditions may change, but too often, we don't. As a result, our knowledge can grow stale. The publishers who questioned *The Independent* informed their thinking and found their best practices using conventional wisdom, and as a result, they either fell behind or missed out on the savings and sales that *The Independent* generated. Let this story be a warning to us all: we shouldn't let a false sense of certainty about knowing "the" answer prevent us from seizing new opportunities. In our efforts to close the gap between average and exceptional work, we shouldn't base our decisions on whatever feels most common.

On the other hand, we shouldn't base our decisions on whatever seems newest, either. This is the second way we often look for best practices: We obsess over trendy tactics. We herald the arrival of a new technology or technique as the latest and greatest approach. *Surely, it will deliver us to the promised land.* We like being "on the bleeding edge," and we love hearing predictions about what the future holds. Like battle cries from the boardroom, we emerge confident in our innovative thinking. *It's the year of mobile! Virtual reality is here!* We glom onto new trends, and we squeeze them for all the value we can before searching for the next one.

Unfortunately, just because something is new doesn't make it the *best* something *for us.* In our hunt for best practices, informing our decisions based purely on the latest or buzziest approaches only biases our thinking toward whatever feels newest. Jumping on the latest bandwagon doesn't ensure we create exceptional work.

The perfect example of conflating "new" with "best" is the rise of SiteLinks. In November 2009, Google introduced SiteLinks, a new feature of its search engine advertising product that would allow marketers to append four additional blue links just below their ads. For instance, if you search "Nike shoes," the subsequent ad might read "Shop Nike.com—Official Nike Store" at the top, followed by four smaller blue links saying something like, "Shop New Releases," "Shop Women's Shoes," "Shop Men's Shoes," and "Shop Children's Shoes." Those last four links are SiteLinks.

As long as I live, I will never forget SiteLinks, or the number Google used to convince advertisers to adopt this feature: 30 percent. That stat is burned into my brain forever. You see, I was part of the sales team at Google that helped launch SiteLinks to advertisers. During beta testing, Google found that clicks to ads increased by "30 percent on average" using SiteLinks—a line I used thousands of times in emails, phone calls, and meetings. As an account manager, I had over 1,000 small business clients, all of which received "scalable sales initiatives" from me and my teammates. Since my clients were small businesses, Google didn't invest in one-on-one or in-person support. Instead, I'd receive spreadsheets and training modules from Mothership Googs, instructing me to send batch emails or pitch decks, or to call a certain subset of accounts to prescribe the same change. In 2009, that change was to enable SiteLinks.

The logic was simple: "We've seen advertisers get 30 percent more clicks on average. If you enable them, you'll also get more clicks. More clicks means more sales on your website." But this was faulty logic, especially considering that small business websites are typically a mess. There's no guarantee they'd see more sales, despite additional traffic. However, there was one thing that was a guarantee: Google would generate more revenue. So I was told to sell SiteLinks.

Despite being in my early twenties, marketing executives and practitioners alike thought I knew something, and I suppose I did know something: I knew what worked on average. As for what might work for my specific clients? That was something I couldn't tell them. I just prayed those questions never came. When they didn't, I was grateful at the time, but now I wonder, why *didn't* they? Why didn't my clients start their thinking by considering their context first, and then make sense of this new trend, given what they knew to be true about their own businesses?

Instead, history repeated with SiteLinks, just as it had with every sale we made. Clients conflated what works in general with what works for them. In under a year, millions of businesses had adopted SiteLinks. Google had activated its massive reach and unleashed legions of charismatic salespeople (and also me) upon their clients, and they simply brute-forced a new trend into existence.

Why are SiteLinks a best practice? Because Google wants them to be.

Months later, when clients complained that their budgets were drained without seeing corresponding sales, I was told to ask if they'd tried Google Analytics on their sites. Google laughed all the way to the bank while I stared at my sales quota and felt sick to my stomach: 104 percent to target.

Like the newspaper publishers that doubted *The Independent* or my clients that trusted Google, in our efforts to get better results, we often seek best practices through conventional wisdom or trendy new tactics. This biases our thinking toward whatever is most common or newest. But there's a third, equally dangerous way we sometimes conduct ourselves at work: we thrash.

All too often, our behavior reveals that we have no idea what we're trying to do. Like Mike Brown, we try absolutely anything and everything until our work devolves into chaos. We send or receive panicked emails. (*What's our Snapchat strategy?!*) We slap more logos on our website and add more skills to our LinkedIn profiles. We run reports to show others all the projects we finished or "pieces" we published or tickets we answered or updates we shipped. In this frenetic and exhausting race for better results, we try lots and lots of stuff without really knowing why.

There's just one problem here. (Actually, no, there are at least twenty-three problems here.) Just because we're doing lots of stuff doesn't mean any of that stuff is the *best* stuff *for us*. Additionally, the more stuff we do, the harder it becomes to identify what's working and what needs fixing. In our desire to see better results, we can get so overwhelmed, stressed, or confused that we simply churn out more. In doing so, we bias our work toward activities, not results or fulfillment. We prioritize tactics over strategy. This rarely, if ever, leads to exceptional work.

Unfortunately, this lack of clarity is enabled by the very things that are supposed to deliver clarity in the first place. Who hasn't gone down a rabbit hole of searches, videos, pages, podcasts, and posts? The internet age has a dark side in our work: Advice Overload. It's just so tempting and easy to seek our answers elsewhere that we find ourselves with far too many of them, far too quickly.

For example, maybe you're a big brand executive and want to capitalize on a new trend—something like predictive analytics. To get your team up to speed, you can simply visit YouTube and pull up tens of thousands of videos from experts. In seconds, you've accessed millions of hours of advice that you and your team can use.

Maybe you're not an executive. Maybe you're just entering the workforce looking for a job, or you're trying to switch career paths, or you're seeking that next promotion. If that's you, why not visit Amazon and buy any of the 47,046 books offering career advice, many from the world's biggest names in business and self-help?

Maybe you love your current job, but you're trying to grow your company's Twitter following. Well, when should you send out your tweets? Quick, can you tell me the best time for a business to tweet?

Time's up, but it doesn't matter if you knew the answer anyway, because in under a second, you can get 35 million results on Google. Even better, you won't need to read any of those pages. You can just glance at the little box at the top that Google uses to share the most popular answers on their search results pages. (Apparently, you should tweet at 3 p.m. local time.)

My friend, this world is flooded with advice and ideas for our work, all of which we can access in an instant—but so can everyone else. And guess what happens when I tell the readers of this book that the best time to tweet is 3 p.m.? That is *no longer* the best time to tweet!

My point is this: it has never been easier to be average. If we don't have an answer or an idea, we can find and follow everyone else's. As a result, much of our work is derivative. Like Mike Brown, we may not want to build average careers or companies, but when we purely rely on the ideas and answers of others, we wind up creating commodity work. It's like someone injected every searcher and every thinker with some Death Wish Coffee, straight to the brain. The world's information has exploded, and we can access it in the blink of a (very twitchy) eye.

THE WHEEL

It's like we're trapped. We're trapped in this never-ending cycle of best practices. It's like this constantly spinning wheel. The character Daenerys Targaryen from *Game of Thrones* nails it when she says the ruling families of her world, Westeros, are all "just spokes on a wheel." First one is on top, then another's on top, and on and on this wheel spins. We might not live in Westeros (thank God—it's pretty murdery there), but we're similarly caught on our own version of that ever-spinning wheel. First one best practice is on top, then another, and another. We just keep hoping and praying that we'll find one to save us. But they're merely spokes on a wheel.

When we base our decisions on conventional wisdom, we're just clinging to one spoke and risk getting crushed as the world turns. When we rely too much on new trends, we stretch ourselves thin, reaching across the wheel to grab the next spoke, then the next, never fully grasping anything, constantly reacting to everything we see coming. When we lack clarity, our work devolves into chaos as the wheel spins out of control.

On and on this wheel spins, taking us to the one place we don't want our careers or companies to be: average.

In my decade as a content marketer, I've watched as my peers and leaders obsessed over banner advertising, then organic search (SEO), then paid search. Before long, it was all about social media, then content marketing, then influencer marketing. As I write these very words, the industry is abuzz about account-based marketing and artificial intelligence. Every year, we write predictions of what the next twelve months will bring, and every year, I wait for someone to admit, "It depends."

Instead, people claim to know "the" answer in some general sense.

It's time we got specific. We're told best practices work best for others, but what works best for *us*? Better yet, what works for *you*? Admittedly, it's not an easy question to answer, especially when we're constantly pressured to deliver results. But we shouldn't make decisions based on whatever is most common or newest. We should make decisions based on whatever works best for us. There's a certain clarity and subsequent power that comes with better self-awareness and situational awareness. It's worth our time to investigate this idea further. That's why I was so excited to learn about Mike Brown and Death Wish Coffee. Fundamentally, it's a story of profound awareness. That level of understanding about his own situation helped Mike make the best decisions possible— better than any best practice could provide.

In the coming chapters, we'll meet some remarkable people who questioned the convention, broke from best practices, and refused to settle for good enough. We'll meet the warm but weird social media team working at a dictionary brand and their leader who used a simple statement to turn their boring marketing into a shocking success. We'll talk to a serial entrepreneur who is frustratingly good at noticing simple but powerful truths about the world that we so often miss. We'll meet a man who saved an island by saving a species in a way his peers overlooked for decades—a fella nicknamed "The Parrot Man of the Caribbean."

From the turnaround story of Starbucks in a market where they previously struggled, to one of the most successful side projects of all time, we'll meet a wide range of people who all exhibit the same behavior: rather than rely on best practices, they did what worked best for them. They asked the right questions rather than obsessing over everyone else's right answers. In the end, this helped them do their very best work.

Today more than ever, it's so incredibly easy to be average. But I know you want something more. It's my fiercest belief that exceptional work only happens when we find and follow what makes us an exception. So how do we do that? And can we make it as simple as finding and following the most common, the latest, or the easiest best practice?

I believe we can. It all starts with a single mentality shift. Ask yourself: Will you continue relying on experts or act more like an investigator? Will you blindly trust the next influencer who hands you an answer, or will you try to find your own? If we start our process there, we'd see the wheel for what it is. We'd make better decisions than any best practice can provide. As we head to the next chapter, hold tight to your desire to do more exceptional work. Like Mike Brown did, we're going to turn that vague and burning desire into something specific and concrete. We're going to close that gap between the work we're doing and the work we aspire to do. To paraphrase our fictional friend Daenerys Targaryen, we're not going to merely stop the wheel.

We're going to break it.

CHAPTER 2

AWARENESS

Uncle DC speaks the truth.

The former Queens native is not a rapper, but he probably could be. He has more swagger than anyone in the room, and he speaks his mind without hesitation. He tweets quick-hitting thoughts about hard work that hundreds of thousands of fans adore, and if you say something he agrees with, he'll shout, "Boom!" or "No doubt!" When he reflects on his craft, which he does often, he'll refer to a predecessor as an OG—original gangster. He's had a long and successful career, and recently, he made it clear with a chest-thumping, eye-opening decision: he's done with best practices.

Uncle DC is David Cancel, the founder and CEO of marketing software company Drift, based in Boston. Before Drift, he founded four different software companies, selling a few and earning enough personal capital to start investing in other tech startups. David Cancel is tall and thin, and thanks to a clean-shaven head, his dark beard and sideburns look like they're snapped onto his face, LEGO-man style. His typical fresh white sneakers match the shock of gray on his chin in color only.

For one year, in 2013, David Cancel and I were colleagues at the marketing tech company HubSpot. Back then, he wasn't Uncle DC. That nickname came later. In 2013, everybody just called him DC or Cancel. However, what was established already was his signature swagger. It was enough to create a certain aura around the man. He arrived at HubSpot in 2011 when the company acquired Cancel's fourth startup, Performable. He was then named chief product officer and asked to fix a terrible problem. HubSpot's software platform, which helps small businesses with their blogging, social media, email, and website analytics, was hemorrhaging customers.

According to legend (and a few designers who survived to tell me the tale), Cancel spent his first few weeks at HubSpot barely talking to anyone. He just sat there, arms folded, watching his team work. Every so often, he'd check the projects of a designer or developer, but mostly, he just watched. Then, after a few weeks, he unceremoniously fired and replaced most of the team. Over time, by improving the design, features, and system for getting customer feedback, Cancel and his new team rebuilt the product and helped fix the company's customer churn problem. Thanks in large part to this effort, HubSpot experienced a successful IPO and, at the time of this writing, is now worth over $4.8 billion.

Like I said: Uncle DC speaks the truth.

THE RISE AND FALL OF A BEST PRACTICE

In 2014, David Cancel left HubSpot to launch Drift, which helps marketers and salespeople chat with website visitors in real time. In the process, he had to swallow perhaps the toughest truth of his career. He looked around at the digital marketing industry—an industry that he helped shape—and he was horrified. He spent a couple of years tinkering on the Drift product and building an initial team before deciding to attack the terrible marketing trends he saw. So one morning, in the spring of 2016, he called up his lone marketer at the time, Dave Gerhardt, with a shocking request.

The first shock to Gerhardt's system was that his CEO, a lifelong engineer and technophile, had actually called him. "A phone call? I'm going to see him in like an hour," Gerhardt later wrote in a blog post about the interaction. If Cancel was placing an actual telephone call, he knew it must be important.

"You got a second?" Cancel asked. "I think we should get rid of all of our forms."

To the non-marketer, this may sound innocuous. To a digital marketer, however, it's like asking them to cut off their left foot—and then to keep jogging.

"Here's B2B marketing 101," Gerhardt explained to me on an episode of *Unthinkable*. "Step one, drive people to your website. Step two, once people are on your website, get them to fill out a form. Step three, after they fill out the form, nurture them, which means spam the hell out of them until they buy from you, unsubscribe, or die."

Welcome to marketing, circa 2016, where two trends smashed together to create one very ubiquitous best practice: the forced form.

The first trend was the rapid rise of content marketing— brands publishing educational or entertaining content to grow an audience, much like a media company would. The second trend was the creation and adoption of a wide array of digital tracking and analytics tools, which meant more chief marketing officers expected every tactic to show direct, measurable conversions and results.

Sitting at the intersection of these two trends was the website form. If you were a marketer who published educational or entertaining content, and if you were asked to show the results from that content in leads or sales, you would often require website visitors to "pay" for your content by submitting their emails and other personal information. Marketers could then track whether those individuals became customers.

Here's how this works: A marketing team publishes a larger piece of content, like an e-book called *The Ultimate Guide to Facebook Advertising*, for instance. They'd then publish several blog posts about the same topic, sharing practical tips or expert interviews about Facebook advertising. These blog posts would drive traffic since articles rank on search engine results pages and often get shared to social networks by readers. Once traffic (i.e., people) arrived to the company site through those blog posts, they'd see a call-to-action to download the full e-book that had inspired the article. ("Did you like this article? Are you ready to become a Facebook advertising master? Download our Ultimate Guide for free.") But there's a catch. To access that meatier piece of content, a reader would be forced to fill out a form asking for contact information. This might include their name, email, job title, company, phone number, and budget. Thus, readers would get their content, and the company would get a new lead that they could proudly say arrived directly from their work.

"Forms are how I get leads," Gerhardt told me. "I love

figuring out how to get more of those leads through things like content upgrades, downloadable guides, email courses, pop-ups, and more." So if you're a marketer like him and suddenly your CEO asks you to remove every one of those forms, naturally, you'd be more than a little stressed.

"I was silent," Gerhardt explained. "[Using forms] was working for us."

In 2016, just the thought of publishing content as a B2B marketer *without* forms was insane. Some might say unthinkable.

Not to Uncle DC.

"Marketing has lost its way," Cancel told Gerhardt on that surprise phone call. "We've lost the importance of [telling] a great story and truly connecting with people. We live in this world where it's all about content, content, and more content. And SEO. And ranking for this keyword and that keyword. And algorithms and conversion rate optimization."

By starting with tactics instead of understanding why those tactics were effective, marketers began to treat people like leads. In doing so, they lost sight of the true goal of using content and the real reason it works in the first place: when you add value to someone's life, they're more likely to reciprocate with attention, trust, and action. Unfortunately, many marketers want to force the issue, which only annoys prospects and customers. As more companies reported initial success using forced forms, more marketers began to adopt the tactic, focusing on the forms themselves, rather than the creation of valuable content. The goal became "get people to fill out the form" rather than "deliver content so good people would pay for it by filling out a form." As it so often happens, that subtle difference made all the difference in the world.

By focusing more on the forms than the value provided to readers, marketers started asking their audience to fill out even more fields. The number of blog posts a company published also increased, which often led to a decrease in quality. The mad dash to generate more traffic had begun. E-books and whitepapers and other high-value types of content became cheap commodities as every competitor in a given niche promised their prospects the "ultimate" or "definitive" or "exhaustive" guide to something. If everyone has the final say, does anyone have any say? (A quick Google search for "ultimate guide to Facebook advertising," in quotes, reveals 139,000 results. Even on YouTube, I found 787 videos. So, sure, they're all "guides." As for that word "ultimate," not so much.) The job of a B2B marketer became a constant battle to add more names into a database—with little accountability for whether they were the right names in the first place.

In the words of Uncle DC: "Marketing today has become more about gaming the system and get-rich-quick-schemes."

Like I said, Uncle DC speaks the truth. And quite frankly, this truth was long overdue in the marketing industry. By the time Cancel founded Drift, marketers had been relying on gated content for almost a decade, since 2006. That was the year that one company often credited with sparking the trend was founded. It was a company later revered and, eventually, criticized for its marketing prowess; a company that would teach an industry about the power of forced forms and, whether intentionally or not, inspire thousands of marketers to start gaming the system.

A company called HubSpot.

"I've created marketing and sales software for so long," Cancel explained. "Now I look back at all of it, and I'm trying to right the world."

After that fateful phone call between Cancel and Gerhardt, the latter responded to his CEO's request. He set all their content free, getting rid of every forced form.

"Not 'get rid of.' We killed them. They're dead," Cancel later told the world on his *Seeking Wisdom* podcast, a show that he hosts with the now-vice president of marketing, and the leader of a growing team of marketers—the one and only Dave Gerhardt. It seems marketing at Drift has been thriving ever since they made what some might call a radical decision. However, to hear Cancel explain his reasoning is to hear a logical, level-headed argument laid out.

He realized that people hate forms. He realized *he* hated forms. Nobody wants to be treated like a "lead" or to give away tons of information to get some commodity content in return. Furthermore, today's buyers are savvier than ever. They have total control over how and where they spend their time. In a world of infinite choice, companies must deliver better experiences—because that's what we as consumers choose. We all want exceptional content *before* sharing any information, not after. We want a brand to add value to our lives before they ask for value from us. Marketers had this backwards.

In addition to this realization, Cancel aspired to grow a massive, modern business. Companies he admired who had done so in the software industry all shared one common trait: passionate audiences. They didn't just have a big list of followers. They had superfans. They proactively built their brands by sharing information freely rather than forcing audiences to fill out forms or acting like most slow-moving B2B companies from decades past. Think of Slack, the fastest-growing B2B tech company ever, or MailChimp, which never raised venture capital but has built a business that generates more than $400 million in annual revenue. Cancel aspired to build a billion-dollar company with Drift, and to do so, he focused on building a passionate, loyal audience. Audiences are made up of people. People hate forms.

"So I said, 'Fuck that. We've got to kill all these things. I have to get Dave on the phone.'"

That's Uncle DC for you. He speaks the truth.

Why don't we?

PIKE SYNDROME

Unlike David Cancel, we seem to leave inner thoughts or gut feelings unspoken. I was a content marketer for more than a decade, and every time I'd discuss forced forms with my peers, we'd all agree that, personally, we couldn't tolerate the things. I mean, who enjoys being offered something "ultimate," only to find out it's one of thousands just like it? Who wants the bait-and-switch feeling of being promised a "free" e-book, template, or report, only to discover you need to fork over all your personal information first?

For years, despite most marketers agreeing that forms were terrible in theory, they didn't do anything about this awfulness. Few spoke up. Unlike David Cancel and Dave Gerhardt, many of us struggle to *trust* our own observations and feelings of the world—especially if it clashes with a best practice. It can feel so hard to do that, but people like Cancel and Gerhardt make it seem so easy. After all, they didn't have some brilliant new idea or uncover a complex new theorem. They informed their decisions with some rather basic observations, and they felt confident enough in those insights to execute differently than others. In the end, when David Cancel's instincts have clashed with industry dogma throughout his long career, he routinely bets on the former, not the latter. Why don't we?

I think we have Pike Syndrome.

There's an old experiment, which is now more of an allegory, that helps explain our temptation to trust conventional thinking rather than our own. Imagine a pike swimming around an aquarium. He's a lithe, ruthless hunter, with rows of razor-sharp teeth sticking up from a menacing underbite. This fish looks perpetually pissed off. If you drop some minnows into the tank, the pike will immediately snap them up. However, if you lower those minnows into the tank inside a glass cup, something different happens. The pike can't see the glass, so he just starts smashing into it again and again in a hopeless pursuit of his prey. He might do this for hours until he eventually concludes that he can't eat the minnows. Then, something amazing happens. You can remove the glass, and the minnows can swim freely around the tank, undisturbed by the pike. Tasty little morsels can swim right in front of his nose, but that perpetually pissed off predator won't move so much as an inch.

The pike has fallen victim to a phenomenon known as "learned helplessness." The theory, often attributed to American psychologist Martin Seligman, describes a condition in which a person (or fish) suffers from a sense of powerlessness as a result of traumatic events or persistent failure. For example, a student who repeatedly fails might conclude that he's a bad student, and thus feel helpless to change his results, which only perpetuates further failure and further convinces him that he's a bad student. Similarly, a designer who continually has her ideas shot down by peers or bosses may assume that she's simply not creative or not good at convincing others, and thus revert to the safer, more conventional approach to each new project. In each case, the subject is conditioned to accept the same falsehood: "I can't. I'm lacking. I'm helpless."

Like the pike, I think many of us suffer from a bit of learned helplessness in our careers. I don't think you and I are blind to the details of the world around us. Neither was the pike. Unfortunately, also like the pike, we've stopped looking. We seek answers externally from people who "know better," whether they operate in the present or succeeded in the past. *I can't possibly know better than them. They're the experts. They're more experienced.* Even if we disagree with the tactic, as with the forced form, we conclude that there must be some hidden knowledge that we lack. We've learned to be helpless like the pike instead of self-empowered like Cancel and Gerhardt.

As a result, we often repeat the convention, glom onto the trend, or spin out of control attempting everything others claim will work. This problem of learned helplessness has only compounded and spread to more people thanks to the internet. More than ever before, endless amounts of best practices are instantly accessible—the answer must be in there somewhere, right? We can't possibly believe that our simple observations of the world around us can hold as much power.

David Cancel's story suggests otherwise.

"Every context is slightly different," he told me. "History rhymes; it doesn't repeat. So you have to be able to walk into a new context, put your experience aside for a bit, and understand what's different."

Just because you failed a test before doesn't mean you

can't succeed in school. Just because your boss disagreed with your ideas doesn't mean you're not creative. History rhymes; it doesn't repeat. The little differences can make all the difference in the world. Unfortunately, most people want to come into a situation and say, "*This* was the playbook over here, so it's the same now." That rarely works, because everything is slightly different, and you have to be open to that.

That understanding and openness helped David Cancel conclude that he needed to remove (sorry—*kill*) every forced form on the Drift website. In doing so, the company set their most valuable content free. They bet more on their own understanding of themselves and their customers than on the most widely used approach in B2B content marketing. On the Drift website, readers still saw an option to subscribe, but it was no longer required. At the bottom of each piece they publish, Drift places a single line of copy that reads, "P.S. Can we send you an email? Once a week or so we send an email with our best content. We never bug you; we just send you our latest piece of content."

Over the next few months, this fifteen-person startup with one marketer named Dave rapidly grew their audience. After removing their forced forms and switching to that optional link, they more than doubled their email list. They brought in five hundred new subscribers per month, compared to the two hundred they'd averaged in previous months. They grew their customer base by 30 percent each month for several months. Next, they wrote a blog post called "Why We're Throwing Out All of Our Lead Forms and Making Content Free," and dozens of industry blogs and thought leaders syndicated and shared the story. David Cancel and Dave Gerhardt appeared on some of the biggest podcasts in their industry too.

On social media, fans came pouring out of the woodwork with visceral, vocal support of what Drift had done. One marketer and new Drift fan wrote, "Dave, you just wrote what every marketer thinks every day when we make a new form. I hate pages that won't let me go further with the content and the company if I want to do it."

Josh Pigford, the founder of analytics tech company Baremetrics, tweeted: "This article/convo from @davegerhardt and @dcancel got me thinking. We were too focused on increasing subscriber counts instead of increasing love for the stuff we're creating."

One blogger and small business owner, Nat Eliason, went so far as to write his own article about why he, too, would remove all forced forms from his site. He then emailed that article to his 10,000 subscribers. According to Gerhardt, most of them had never heard of Drift...until Nat's email.

Today, more than 100,000 businesses use Drift's products.

THE DETAILS CONTAIN MORE THAN JUST THE DEVIL

For Drift, it seems like a simple observation from David Cancel sparked a movement. But the observation was just the first step. In reality, his willingness to act on it made all the difference. We notice things about our situation all the time. Just as the pike sees the minnows but doesn't take action, we see things unfolding around us every day with our teams, our customers, our industry, and more. It's all there, floating right by us—if only we'd reach out and use it.

"It's always been there," Cancel told me. "But somehow, we've all become too smart for our own good. We think, 'Oh, no, we need some profound idea or some view of the market so that I don't have to go through that process of learning about the world again.'"

There's always something missing from any conventional tactic or strategy: the specifics of your context. When we compare and contrast a real-world situation full of nuance and variables to any general advice, the latter rarely feels like a complete plan. Sometimes, all it takes is a single detail pulled from the world right around you to shatter the illusion that a best practice is indeed the best path for us.

"It's funny because I never thought of removing our forms before," Gerhardt said on an episode of Drift's podcast. "But once [Cancel] pointed it out to me, I instantly said yes, right away, and it wasn't because it was my boss telling me to do something. It's because I thought, 'Wait a second, this makes *perfect* sense.'"

That "wait a second" feeling echoed around the marketing industry after Drift made their decision. One of the blogs that covered the news was ChiefMartec, run by Scott Brinker—an influential site run by an influential marketing leader. In his coverage of Cancel's decision, Brinker pointed to a joint study from the Content Marketing Institute and MarketingProfs to highlight just how unthinkable the move seemed at first. The 2016 survey of 1,521 B2B content marketers found that lead generation was their top goal, narrowly edging sales.

"So when David Cancel, Drift's CEO, proposed eliminating all forms in front of the marketing team's content, you can probably imagine Dave's puzzlement. Say what?" Brinker wrote. "As radical of a move as this may seem through the eyes of a marketer, if we put on a prospect's hat—remember, we're all committed to being customer-centric, right?—this actually seems, well, pretty nice. No more lead forms to fill out? No more ~~spam~~ nurture emails or phone calls from marketing or sales people, aggressively pushing me toward the next step in their funnel?

I get the content I want, when I want it, without jumping through hoops, and then I decide if and when I want to pursue a closer relationship. That would be pleasant, wouldn't it?"

Indeed it would, Mr. Brinker.

"If you don't pay attention to these subtle differences and details, then you're going to try to emulate everybody else," Cancel said. "That doesn't work." Not if you want to be exceptional. In fact, I'd go so far as to say that some marketers shouldn't emulate David Cancel. The point isn't to reject an old convention in favor of a new one. Marketers shouldn't merely replace forced forms with links reading "P.S.—Can I send you an email?" No, the lesson Cancel's story reveals is that we need to get better at getting better. We need to constantly admit that our thinking must be updated and revised on an ongoing basis. As soon as we believe we've found "the" answer, we're at risk of getting complacent and shipping commodity work. Instead, in constantly updating our understanding of the world, we'd act like investigators rather than experts. We'd focus our efforts hunting for evidence and challenging assumptions instead of relying on generalities or false absolutes.

This all starts with admitting that what we "know" is likely just an assumption. Unfortunately, something prevents us from doing so.

"The issue is pride, and the byproduct of pride is stubbornness," he said.

Even when helpful information sits right in front of our noses, we prefer to have "the" answer in some absolute sense. That might originate in past work or arrive in a neatly packaged list of tips and tricks from our favorite experts. Regardless, when we feel we have "the" answer, we stop looking for new details to update our thinking. We know the best practice, so the learning phase of our process is over. It's time to execute.

That's a dangerous way to operate.

"I'm always quoting [Berkshire Hathaway investor and vice chairman] Charlie Munger when he says, 'I'd rather be vaguely right than precisely wrong,'" Cancel said. (The quote was originally credited to British economist John Maynard Keynes. It has since been referenced in connection with Munger, and it's become a sort of mantra for the legendary investor.)

"Who cares if you're right or wrong?" Cancel said. "The goal isn't to be right or wrong in business. The goal is to serve the customer."

Now here's the tough pill to swallow: that kinda sucks. It's *so* satisfying to be right in theory, now and forever, rather than to constantly course-correct. Imagine if I could write this book by following "The 10 Secrets to Writing a Bestselling Book from the World's Best Authors" rather than spending years of iterating, learning, and making mistakes. As the snow outside my window in Queens is driven sideways by the wind and I labor through this chapter, I'd feel oh-so-warm and fuzzy if I could start and stop my thinking with a precise list of steps to follow.

Ever the blunt bringer of truth, David Cancel doesn't believe that's ever possible. The best a best practice can bring you are possibilities, but then you have to vet those possibilities using that body of knowledge you have on the world around you. There are no final answers—only lifelong learning.

At a recent speaking event, Cancel said this idea became crystal clear when he was asked a simple question by a young entrepreneur: "How should I communicate my company's upcoming pivot to my investors?"

"I realized I no longer think about making pivots that way," Cancel remembered. The entrepreneur was implying that there was one single moment of pivoting the company in a big way looming in his future, and his stress was a symptom of his upcoming, wide-ranging shift. Cancel decided to diagnose the illness. "The goal is to make micro-adjustments every day so you never have to make the big pivot later."

To help explain this idea of being vaguely right, Cancel cites Lookery, one of his former companies, which he founded in late 2007. The business helped marketers target their customers on social media based on demographic information. Cancel admits that, back then, he acted like that young entrepreneur—overconfident and proud. He and his cofounders at Lookery had a grand vision for exactly the analytics product they wanted to build, so they rarely, if ever, interviewed users for feedback to make adjustments. A couple years later, with the company on the brink of collapse, they were forced to radically change their design to create a product others actually wanted to use. Looking back, Cancel wishes he'd acted less like an expert who knew "the" answer and more like an investigator who found evidence that could inform smaller adjustments.

"The signs are always there," he said, reflecting on the young entrepreneur's question. "But when you have to make a big pivot, it's a sign that you weren't listening all along the way."

After absorbing past mistakes trying to be overly precise and prescriptive, Cancel is instead building Drift on the idea of lifelong learning. So far, so good. As of 2018, the company has a team of 130 across offices in Boston and San Francisco. Just seven months after raising $32 million in a Series B round of VC funding, Drift announced an additional $60 million Series C in April 2018, thanks to a reported 10x increase in revenue between 2017 and 2018. Drift now produces multiple podcasts and video series, in addition to hosting multiple annual events attended by thousands of passionate fans—fans who wear Drift t-shirts and download wallpapers for their phones with pictures of Cancel's favorite quotes. The quotes, like their source, speak the truth. Because that's what Uncle DC does. He doesn't predict the future. He doesn't "innovate." He sees the world exactly as it is, and he has the confidence and clarity to act accordingly.

What if we did too?

In our journey to do more exceptional work, best practices are the supposed "right answers" we're told to follow. But in reality, people who do exceptional work like David Cancel and Mike Brown seem to recognize that "the" answer will change. They know they can never complete their learning process, so they master the ability to find their own answers, constantly revising their thinking with details pulled out from their unique environments. They refuse to operate in the abstract.

"To cite Charlie Munger again, who I love—yes, I have a man-crush on a ninety-five-year-old dude—but the craziest thing is that, with every year that passes, I'm able to reflect back and realize that I actually know less than I thought," Cancel said.

In many ways, like their CEO, Drift's entire team exudes a certain swagger. They have total confidence in their mission and vision. They seem to beat their chests about the movement they're building, and they call out unspoken truths whenever they spot problems in the sales, marketing, and customer support professions. Even the little things showcase their swagger. They share pithy maxims from business legends on social media; they drop a mean bass before every episode of their podcast...and they also don't say things like "drop a mean bass." This software-as-a-service brand is all about confidence. (Can "SaaS" mean Swagger-as-a-Service? No? Okay, let's just move on.)

Drift projects a confidence bordering on egotistical, but in another sense, the team is doing something rather humble: they're building a company on the notion that they don't have any answers. They understand their ideas may be wrong and that their knowledge must constantly be updated. They're ruthless hunters of those little details swimming all around them.

"I go back to first principles, a.k.a. grandmother's wisdom," Cancel said. "If we want to build a product that people actually want to use, why don't we just ask the people? If we want to sell our product to more customers, why don't we just talk to them when they visit our website?"

This approach to user testing and speaking directly with customers has led the company to move beyond their initial chat-bot product to include new features like Drift Email, which uses past conversations between a company and its prospects to prevent others from receiving canned or generic emails that no longer make sense.

Speaking directly with customers also informs Drift's branding. They've named their category, calling their movement "conversational marketing," which according to Drift's website, is "the process of having real-time, one-to-one conversations in order to capture, qualify, and connect with your best leads. Unlike traditional marketing, conversational marketing uses targeted messaging and intelligent chat-bots instead of lead capture forms."

Additionally, some of the world's best venture capital firms trusted this movement enough to invest in Drift, as firms like Sequoia Capital, NextView Ventures, General Catalyst, and CRV have all added millions to the company's coffers. Drift has even attracted a few rather auspicious angel investors: the founding executives of HubSpot.

Cancel credits all of it to the company's willingness to get closer to the customer and to base their decisions on what they learn, regardless of the conventional approach. That, he argues, is reasoning from first principles: a business exists to serve customers. Why not focus more on that?

This thinking doesn't only apply to newer startups or B2B businesses, either. Just ask Finn Dowling, who operates in a very traditional, slow-moving industry, with very little budget.

MEET EDDIE THE TERRIBLE

Finn is a writer and marketer at the Humane Society Silicon Valley (HSSV), a nonprofit animal shelter started in 1929, and it was there that Finn faced a big problem in the form of a little dog named Eddie.

"He came to us as a stray, and he was pretty nutters right from the get-go," Finn said. "But he was a lot of show and no go when it came to aggression, meaning he barked and snapped but never actually bit anybody."

Still, this blonde Chihuahua mixed breed would be a tough sell to prospective parents:

- He hated other dogs.
- He loved children, but mostly just their fingers.
- He barked uncontrollably whenever left alone in his crate.
- He tore every item he could get his little mouth on into complete shreds.

"This is something that shelters see a lot—small dogs acting absolutely terrified and acting like serial murderers," Finn said. As a result of his behavior, that troublesome little dog earned the nickname "Eddie the Terrible."

For two years, the HSSV struggled to find Eddie a new home. That gnashing ball of teeth and fur simply didn't fit into the traditional tropes shelters use to promote their animals. Perhaps you've experienced what I mean firsthand. Maybe you're watching your favorite TV show or are about to view a seemingly harmless YouTube video. You're minding your own damn business, when suddenly—*BAM!*—a pair of big, brown, sad eyes are blinking at you from inside a metal cage. Next comes a one-eyed cat struggling to clean her tangled fur. Now here's a nervous little mutt sitting alone in the dirt, shaking spastically like he's telling you, "Man, I've seen some *stuff* in my life." And then, the Guilt Trip *Coup de Grace*: the haunting, tear-inducing lyrics of a Sarah McLachlan song start to play (*In the aaaarms of an aaaangel!*) and, wait a second, is that actually Sarah McLachlan? With a dog on her lap? Begging you to act now to save these animals...or else?

Damn. Aren't pets supposed to be awesome?

"Most shelter marketing makes me want to stick my head in an oven," Finn said. Traditionally, shelters have been so strapped for resources that they never stop to wonder if the typical approaches are actually effective. Instead, they mimic what they see other shelters doing, like running depressing TV ads or (another common tactic) writing overly effusive articles about a pet. You know the one: "Fluffy just needs a family to love him. He's had a rough past, but he enjoys belly rubs and snuggles and kisses and *isn't he just the cutest wittle thing?!*" Every single shelter seems to use the same exact playbook. You might say that the stress of dealing with all those pets turns volunteers into a bunch of copy*cats*.

(Eh? *Ehhh?*)

Right. Head, meet oven. Let's move on...

For decades, the HSSV ran that standard playbook, but then along came Eddie. It would have been an outright lie to talk about Eddie in overly effusive terms. He wasn't a sympathetic character. If anything, he was the villain. You don't feel sorry for a dog like that. You feel sorry for whoever ends up with the bastard. After two years of struggling to find this little beast a new home, Finn knew they had to try something radical. "We decided that we would market him as the absolute worst dog in the world."

The next day, she wrote an article called, "A Full Disclosure Blog: Three Reasons You DON'T Want to Adopt Eddie the Terrible." The post included some unusual selling tactics.

"Like to go for walks in dog infested areas? Enjoy the dog park? Keep walking. He goes from zero to Cujo in .05 seconds when he sees another dog on leash."

The post continued: "Want your kids to grow up with a full complement of fingers and toes? Not the dog for you."

The article included graphics superimposing Eddie onto the posters of various TV shows. One reads, "The Walking Ed," while another says, "Nightmare on Ames Avenue" (the street where the HSSV is located). My personal favorite shows a familiar green background with wisps of white vapor as if from a science experiment. On the right side sits Eddie, ears up, mouth hanging open. In the middle, some letters in squares that resemble the periodic table of elements, and the parody title: "Adopting Bad."

After publishing the piece, Finn met her team at a company Christmas party. The group had a particularly long day, and they were relieved to unwind and celebrate together. Then they got an unexpected call. *Good Morning America* had seen the article. They were sending a producer to the shelter. They'd be there in fifteen minutes.

Once their interview aired the next week, the floodgates opened. *ABC News*, *USA Today*, *The Daily Mail*, *CBS*, *Inside Edition*, *The Huffington Post*, and *People* all came calling. The blog post continued to gain traction too. It was shared on Facebook over 32,000 times and tweeted over 6,300 times in the first week alone. In total, the story reached an estimated seven million people across every channel and medium as more and more readers, viewers, and listeners fell in love with that fiery little furball. Best of all, after two years of being overlooked in the shelter, two years without finding parents to love him, Eddie the Terrible found a home in just two days.

"He was adopted by a couple with no kids and no dogs," Finn explained. "He's still a jerk in public, but not a dangerous jerk."

Eddie's adoptive dad is retired and his wife works part time, leaving plenty of room in their lives for the little dog with the big personality. The last Finn heard, Eddie's new dad, who has some disabilities, even wants to get him registered as a therapy dog to take him more places.

For such a terrible dog, Eddie has a wonderful life.

VISION (BUT NOT THE KIND WE IMAGINE)

In every article they publish today, the HSSV blog reflects that witty and refreshing style first found in the article about Eddie. Finn has since moved on to work on a new project called "Mutual Rescue," a series of emotional documentary films created by the Humane Society sharing the stories of how adopted pets helped improve or even save the lives of their new owners. The films aim to increase annual donations to pet shelters by helping people see how animal causes are people causes too. Rescuing a pet's life can rescue a human's life. It's mutual.

Today, both Finn and the movement she supports are thriving, while Eddie continues to get all the love he can handle at home. It's a wonderful story. But when we return to our own work, it's easy to conclude that things aren't quite so simple or rosy for us. We want better results but aren't sure how to get them. We want to feel more fulfilled but can't simply write a magical blog post to change our fortunes. We still face this gap between what we're doing now and what we aspire to do—the gap between average and exceptional.

Ugh.

Reading success stories can be equal parts inspiring and frustrating. The David Cancels of the world encourage us to do better work, while at the same time, their stories make their work seem effortless. *Just remove your website forms! Just write a sarcastic blog post! Then, POOF! You'll see great results.*

Somehow, the protagonists of success stories never seem to fall victim to that endless wheel of conventional thinking that can confound or even cripple us in our work.

Finn has strong feelings about trying to copy anyone else's recipe for success. "That's not where you start. Particularly with marketing or anything creative, you don't try to replicate it. You try to smash it on the ground, pick it apart, maybe see if there's something that works in it, and then rebuild something completely different."

The people we've met so far in these pages seem to view the gap between average and exceptional work through a different lens than others. When they imagine what it takes to do amazing work, most people picture some kind of hellscape to cross. It's like they're actively looking for reasons why it's too hard. "Yeah, it'd be great to be *over there* instead of staying right here, but, look, there are all these rocks and snakes and—wait a second, have we considered what we're going to do about all that molten lava? We need a case study! We need an all-hands! Give me the blueprint! And anyway, even if we get past that, there are bear traps to walk over and barbed wire to crawl under and laser beams to dance around. Yanno, on second thought, no thanks. I'm good right here. Let's just keep doing the tried-and-true, thank you very much."

Then we hear about people like Finn Dowling, David Cancel, and Mike Brown, and they seem to look at the same terrain and laugh. "Rocks? Snakes? Lava? What are you talking about? This looks awesome!" They go skipping through what they see as a big green field, and they sing "Zip-a-Dee-Doo-Dah" on their way to doing more work that everyone else only wishes they could do.

What the actual heck? Are their stories pure fantasy, or can we learn from them in the very real world we call home? How can we see our careers like they see theirs?

Our first step is to consider that the ability to innovate doesn't require the type of vision we normally assign to our heroes. Because instead of peering into the future, the people we've met so far have the uncanny ability to observe the world around them as it is right now.

Mike Brown of Death Wish Coffee and the publishers at *The Independent* didn't gaze into a crystal ball to make their decisions. Mike talked to customers. *The Independent* adapted to their current internet-enabled era. Likewise, David Cancel and Finn Dowling didn't benefit from some sort of magical gift of foresight. They both had more empathy for those on the receiving end of their work than their peers did.

I don't think innovators see the future. Consider instead that their real advantage is their ability to, well, *consider* things. In this way, I suppose they do have a certain kind of "vision," in that they see the world more clearly than most.

There's so much information bombarding us, so many experts telling us what we "have to" do, and so much pressure to deliver results in our work, that we start to doubt our ability to deliver. We struggle with learned helplessness, and we inform our decisions using generalized advice or past precedents rather than our own investigation of the world around us. We model ourselves after the success stories we admire. Unfortunately, a funny thing happens when we try to *resemble* success: we usually don't find it. We wind up looking like everyone else. Like copy machines (remember those?), the copy of a copy of a copy never comes out looking the same.

In the internet age, best practices have become table stakes—instantly accessible and ubiquitous knowledge that levels the playing field. We can all find it and copy it. So if that stuff is table stakes, what can separate us? What happens when we aspire to reach that next level in our work?

If the people we've met so far can show us anything, it's the power in focusing more of our time and attention on our specific context than the best practice. After all, you might conclude that using website forms is actually the right approach for your company, given the differences between you and Drift. Or perhaps, given those differences, you might create an entirely new way of generating demand for your business. Both paths are potentially great. What matters isn't the decision itself. What matters in the end is that your decisions are the right ones *for you*.

While best practices masquerade as final answers, they're merely possibilities. Should you remove your website's forms, or should you use them? Should you copy a competitor's sappy marketing tone of voice, or should you do something more sarcastic and irreverent? The answer is always the same: it depends. It depends on your context. Whether we start with our own ideas or the answers handed to us from others, the real trick is to *contextualize* those possibilities. Thus, the question becomes: do you know your context well enough to do so?

THE FOUNDATION OF GREAT WORK

In the industrial age, when most jobs required people to act like commodities and repeat a few behaviors with little differences between individuals, professionals were told what great work required. Today, we have to unlearn that very lesson.

In generations past, because the goal in factories or farms was uniformity and sameness, people learned the foundation of great work was expertise. Know *how* to do the work and do it exactly as prescribed, and you'd have a great career. But in most careers today, when the goal is to solve complex problems and create and invent, the foundation of great work is no longer expertise. It's awareness. To possess the same "vision" of those innovators, to understand our context clearly when we make decisions, we need to develop our sense of self-awareness and situational awareness.

You've likely heard the saying that, if the only tool you

have is a hammer, everything looks like a nail. According to David Cancel, this is how we act when we base our work on expertise. We too readily assume that we know exactly what to do, whether because we've done it before or because we've learned from someone who has.

"If past experience is your hammer," Cancel said, "then in every situation you walk into, you're going to think it's just like every other situation in your career. But it's not true." We have to both contextualize past precedents to our new situation, as well as update our knowledge of the world as it changes.

What if you were to form your own thoughts rather than rely on conventional wisdom? What if you were to spend more time considering the details of your specific context rather than the generally accepted practice? If best practices are merely spokes on an endlessly spinning wheel, then what if we were to escape that cycle entirely to think for ourselves?

Unfortunately, it's a reasonably easy thing to *recognize* the problems with best practices. It's entirely another matter to craft your own. Once we embrace that our context holds crucial information to help us do better work, we need to actually make the right decisions based on what we learn. How do we do that? To ask an even more fundamental question: how can we *trust* that the information we identify in our context is actually worth using?

Well, as it turns out, we each possess a skill for doing this: intuition. Sadly, trusting your intuition just doesn't feel as practical as following a best practice, so that's our next challenge. We're about to meet some of the world's top thinkers and do something that might seem crazy at first. We're going to turn intuition into a tangible weapon we can wield.

We all have the ability to break the wheel and do our best work, but first, we need to find our sledgehammers.

CHAPTER 3

THE SLEDGEHAMMER

Consider the following translations of the opening lines of Homer's epic poem, the *Odyssey:*

Sing in me, Muse, and through me tell the story
Of that man skilled in all ways of contending,
The wanderer, harried for years on end,
After he plundered the stronghold
On the proud height of Troy. (Fitzgerald l.1-5)

Muse, tell me of the man of many wiles
The man who wandered many paths
    of exile. (Mandelbaum l.1-2)

Tell me, Muse, about the man of many turns, who many
Ways wandered when he had sacked
    Troy's holy citadel. (Cook l.1-2)

Sing to me of the man, Muse, the
man of twists and turns
Driven time and again off course,
once he had plundered
The hallowed heights of Troy. (Fagles l.1-3)

For thousands of years, people have called upon the Muse to empower their work. Many ancient Greek poets opened by invoking the deity to do the work for them. The Muse was the actual storyteller; the poet was a mere vessel. After all, the Muse is an ancient being, undying and creatively unbounded, while we humans are small and helpless. What could you, a tiny individual in the infinite cosmos, possibly offer the world? So, we call to the Muse to inspire us. We agonize over finding Her. We beg for Her help and inspiration. In the end, the Muse allows mere mortals like us to do our best work.

I think that's total crap.

I think the Muse is an excuse for why we don't do exceptional work. For thousands of years, people outsourced ownership over their creativity to a mythical being. Today, the Muse has been replaced with other ideas: the guru, the industry expert, the case study, the random moments of inspiration, and of course, the best practice. We fall victim to a false belief that we must locate something "out there" in order to do our best work. As a result, too many people *think* about doing something, instead of actually doing it. By this rationale, it's not our call. It's not on us. We're just "waiting for the Muse to strike." We need to Google the best practice. Or tweet about it. Or watch another video about it. On and on the wheel spins.

Artist Chuck Close once said, "Inspiration is for amateurs. The rest of us just show up and get to work." I tend to agree, but I'd tweak it slightly: inspiration is for those with Pike Syndrome. (I know, I know—my version isn't nearly as fun to share in a graphic on Instagram.) This attack on inspiration is more an attack on how we typically *think* about inspiration: a prerequisite to doing great work. But I think this is a form of Pike Syndrome. We've learned to be helpless instead of self-empowered.

When faced with that endlessly spinning wheel of best practices, it can seem harder to trust our own abilities to think critically and creatively, but if we're going to break the wheel, we have to first unlearn this helplessness. Rather than rely on something "out there" like the Muse or the guru, we have to rely on something we each possess: our intuition.

Unfortunately, in our society, intuition has been grouped together with the Muse. Just reading the word "intuition" might cause you to cringe. *Come on, Jay, I thought this book would be practical and smart. Now you're telling me intuition is the solution?*

Even if you're a believer in the power of intuition, it's still tempting to view it as some kind of magic, as if the Muse had come calling. We think of intuition as gut feelings or lightning-strike moments. I blame the long history of humans trying to understand this phenomenon, and I think we've overlooked a rather simple explanation.

Intuition has been called many things over the years. Albert Einstein (not a guy typically associated with fluffy ideas) once said, "There is no logical way to the discovery of these elemental laws. There is only the way of intuition, which is helped by a feeling for the order lying behind the appearance."

For Einstein, intuition is "our most sacred gift" while the rational mind is "a servant of that gift." Unfortunately, he concluded, we are building a society that values the servant and not the gift.

Some people debate the validity of these statements, questioning whether Einstein actually said them. Regardless, the words themselves are rather encouraging, provided they already align with your preexisting beliefs. I remember first reading them and thinking, "Hell yes! Intuition *is* our gift! We should prioritize it more! Society has it backwards!" But whether you're like me and you love the concept, or you're more skeptical, Einstein's definition still isn't overly useful. It leads to more questions than answers. How do we find "the order lying behind the appearance" anyway? How do we unleash our gift, rather than rely purely on the servant? This feels like waiting around for the Muse again, and I have work to do.

In his bestselling book *Megatrends*, author John Naisbitt provides another take: "Intuition becomes increasingly valuable in the new information society precisely because there is so much data." The book, published in 1982, explores ten different trends that would greatly affect the world for generations to come. When he covers the explosion of information, Naisbitt takes Einstein's definition of intuition one step closer to practical use. While Einstein called it a "feeling for the order lying behind the appearance" of things, Naisbitt describes it as the ability to derive meaning from data. Both men agree: intuition informs the decision-making process by helping you identify an underlying meaning beneath the face value of something. It is the ability to interpret the world you observe, to contemplate or measure it, and to do so quickly.

The idea that we can rapidly make sense of things is discussed most famously in modern society by author Malcolm Gladwell. In his bestseller *Blink*, he writes about "rapid cognition," or snap judgments. We constantly make snap judgments about the world around us, and these moments of rapid cognition can and should inform the actions we take. However, we also feel a tension between our snap judgments and rational thoughts, which prevents us from taking intuition as seriously as we should. Gladwell writes, "We are innately suspicious of this kind of rapid cognition," believing instead that longer and more rigorous research leads to better conclusions. But as he concludes, "decisions made very quickly can be every bit as good as decisions made cautiously and deliberately."

Gladwell has stated publicly that his book is not written in support of or against snap judgements. Some are good and some are bad. The important thing is that we learn to notice them and take them seriously. What matters most is our ability to become more self-aware and situationally aware, thus enhancing our ability to derive meaning from the world. Gladwell wants us to pay more attention to our context, and he believes snap judgments help alert us to those details—if only we knew how to sort the good ones from the bad.

Gladwell's ideas align well with our solution to commodity work: investigating our context to find better answers and ideas. I love the idea of pausing long enough to consider our internal monologue as Gladwell suggests. But what if your inner monologue isn't saying anything? What if it's saying a lot, but you're not sure which of it should actually inform your actions? What if it's wrong? And of course, we have to ask, what if you're under so much pressure at work that finding the time to stop and consider the world around you feels like a damn luxury?

Einstein, Naisbitt, and Gladwell each compel us to take intuition more seriously as a tool in our work—but I don't think we've found our practical definition just yet. We still need something to grasp like a sledgehammer to break the wheel.

All three of these great thinkers agree that intuition is important. It helps us find meaning among the noise. They also agree that we need to take intuition more seriously as we make decisions. Lastly, they acknowledge that society's perception of intuition is often inaccurate, which prevents us from proactively developing and trusting it. Instead, intuition is often misconstrued as a modern form of the mythical Muse. That's a problem, but it's largely one of perception. In reality, the more difficult, more fundamental problem is that we don't know how to *hone* our intuition. Understanding that would then remove the stigma, so we should focus our exploration on how to *use* intuition, more so than how to define it.

Just think: when you truly believe in its power and don't

view intuition as a fluffy ideal, can you even begin to explain how to proactively develop it to someone else? That's our challenge.

So how do we do this?

For starters, we have to find a conscious process that can help us train our intuition. We can't rely on pure happenstance, since that's the Muse all over again, nor can we consider it an entirely subconscious process, since we don't proactively control that. As Gladwell states in *Blink*, we all have a constant "backstage" thought process happening. That's our intuition at work. However, if we're going to deploy that ability in a more on-demand way, we have to learn how to consciously control it. The benefits of intuition seem too great for us not to try.

You've experienced these benefits before, I'm sure. You're doing your work or thinking about your next move, and suddenly, you just *know*. Few things feel better than those moments. Seemingly out of nowhere, we receive Einstein's sacred gift. We draw immediate meaning from all the information around us, just as Naisbitt suggests we should. We experience a snap judgment that feels more like a refreshing moment of brilliance—rapid cognition in the most wonderful of ways. Thus, intuition acts like a sort of "instant clarity generator." These moments are wildly empowering and addictive, but they seem to happen at random. What if we could change that? What if we could control it?

FINDING CLARITY

Gary Klein is a research psychologist famous for his pioneering work in the field of naturalistic decision making. Klein's work seems to align with Gladwell's "rapid cognition" idea when he refers to intuition as subconscious reasoning. In psychology, subconscious reasoning is known as "priming"—past experiences that we hardly noticed which then affect how we make decisions later. We rarely recognize when this happens to us. This is essentially pattern matching, done quickly and subconsciously. You can't say why you know something. You just know.

According to Klein, our ability to recognize patterns in a new situation based on past experiences creates a feeling of instant clarity. In his book *Seeing What Others Don't: The Remarkable Ways We Gain Insights*, he argues that coincidences inform intuition—literally, things that "coincide." Intuition helps you identify the details of one situation that coincide with the details of another.

"Coincidences change our understanding, change what we notice, change what excites us, and set us on the path to making a discovery," Klein writes. "Coincidences can also change our actions. One way they do this is by giving us an idea of what we need to alter to break a pattern we don't like."

By the standard definition, "coincidences" are hard to control, and that interpretation of intuition is not overly useful if we're trying to proactively improve our decision-making skills. If we link intuition and coincidences, it still feels safer, more predictable, and more tangible to rely on a best practice. At first glance, coincidences don't feel much more helpful than the Muse. However, the ability to *identify* coincidences requires a subtle mental shift—one that we'd be wise to understand since this shift is quite practical indeed. Namely, we have to be open to the details of the world around us. If we aren't, we won't recognize patterns or spot those coincidences in the first place. According to Klein, it's the *lack* of openness that plagues so many decisions made in the workplace.

"I still observe executives exhibiting the same lack of courage or knowledge that undercut previous waves of innovation," he writes. "They declare that they want more innovation but then ask, 'Who else is doing it?' They claim to seek new ideas but shoot down every one brought to them."

Just think about the last time somebody shot down your ideas. There's an underlying, if unspoken, set of emotions that leads to the rejection. Fear. Stress. Stubbornness. Laziness. Leaders who are all too quick to shoot down unconventional ideas are implicitly scoffing at Charlie Munger's favorite quote when he encourages us to be "vaguely right." Instead, those fearful, stressed, stubborn, or lazy people around us prefer to be precisely right. They want "the" answer in some absolute sense, but that's about as practical as invoking a Greek deity to give you creative powers. In the end, they merely wind up being precisely wrong more often than not.

Klein quotes Mark Twain, underscoring this point: "You can't depend on your eyes when your imagination is out of focus."

Unlike Einstein, Gladwell, and others, Klein moves us one step closer to grasping our intuition as a tangible tool. To use our "sacred gift," we need to remain more open and sensitive to the specific details of each situation we encounter. (This is part of the reason the stereotypical corporate grindstone removes our intuition as a skill: employees become numb to their environments.)

According to Merriam-Webster Dictionary—a brand whose hilarious story we'll explore later—intuition is defined as "a quick and ready insight." No surprises there, as this aligns with every interpretation we've heard thus far. But let's look beyond the modern definition to the root of the word itself. The word "intuition" comes from the Latin verb *intueri* which means "to consider," or from the late middle English translation, *intuit*, which means "to contemplate." Intuition is not some mythical Muse. It's not merely a backstage process. It's something we can consciously control. As the root of the word suggests, it's our ability to consider or contemplate the world around us. In a workplace flooded with conventional thinking, intuition is *the process of thinking for yourself.*

Not only is this a very practical thing to do at work, but it's something that is in no way reserved for a gifted few. We can all think critically and deeply to consider the world around us (*intueri*). We can all improve how we contemplate our context (*intuit*). It's the remedy to clinging to best practices. It's the sledgehammer to break the wheel. If best practices lead to average work, then average work is merely the failure to contemplate your environment deeply enough.

The difference between many of us and the exceptional individuals we've met so far is their refusal to lapse into autopilot. They remain open to and aware of the details of the world around them. They never stop considering and contemplating things.

- Mike Brown reflected on his career aspirations and also noticed a pattern when speaking with his customers. Starting there, his logic eventually led to Death Wish Coffee, using robusta beans with confidence.

- The publishers at *The Independent* witnessed a rise in internet readership and decline in print purchases. They also realized that broadsheet papers originated in a different time due to different regulations. Thus, they shrank their print papers.

- David Cancel noticed how terrible forced website forms made him feel and realized that a big, loyal, passionate audience would be needed to grow Drift into a huge success. He saw how the buyer had changed, demanding great experiences more than ever. Drift then removed all their forced forms.

- Finn Dowling embraced that Eddie was indeed terrible. She also observed that most animal shelters promoted each pet as if they were either charity cases or perfect angels. In the end, she used both realizations to inform her viral article.

All of these people seemed to either view their environments with more clarity or simply take firsthand details more seriously than most. They considered the world more critically. They constantly used, refined, and trusted their intuition.

How can we do the same? How can we more proactively consider the world around us?

Simple: we need to ask better questions.

When we act like investigators who contemplate the world, we care more about asking the right questions than knowing the right answers. Absolutes or generalizations can only get us so far—perhaps only as far as average. When we ask questions, we admit we don't yet have the answers and go seeking them in the world around us. In other words, we pursue curiosity.

"Curiosities provoke people to investigate further, just as coincidences do," Gary Klein writes. "The initial 'What's going on here?' reaction doesn't contain the insight, but it starts the person on the road to gaining the insight."

Our journey down that road is the journey toward exceptional work. With each step we take, each question we ask, we hone our intuition. But it all starts with the willingness to pursue your curiosity.

THE PEO

For more bashful crowds, Suzy Batiz introduces herself as a CEO. But to her team, she's the PEO. "I'm the Poo Executive Officer," she said. "Because I sell a lot of poo spray."

You read that right: she sells poo spray. Her company

Poo-Pourri generates tens of millions in sales of their odor-blocking products every year. "It's all kind of ridiculous," Suzy said. "I've made millions of dollars selling poo spray. It's like some cosmic joke."

It may sound like a joke, but Suzy takes this business very seriously.

Kind of.

"Our business is to make it smell like your business never even happened!" quips a pretty young woman at the end of a video selling Poo-Pourri. This video, called "Girls Don't Poo," is one of Suzy's early smash hits. It features a beautiful woman talking openly and hilariously about those unmentionable moments. She has bright red hair and wears red lipstick, a pearl necklace, and matching earrings. She looks rather regal, like a Disney princess— only her throne is made of porcelain.

The ad opens to the sound of a toilet flushing from behind a stall. The door swings open, revealing the smirking spokeswoman. "You would not *believe* the motherload I just dropped," she says.

Next, she appears in a few everyday scenarios, lamenting a lingering problem.

"Nothing is worse than stinking up the shared toilet at work, or the toilet at a party, or your lover's apartment."

"Of course, flushing removes the *graphic* evidence, but what can be done of that subtle scent of—" (cut to the woman sitting in a field surrounded by cows) "a three-hundred-cow dairy farm?" (For emphasis, a loud *MOO!*)

"So how do you make the world believe your poop doesn't stink, or that you never poop at all? Poo-Pourri!"

This video has racked up over 250 million views and generated more than $4 million in sales in its first year—backorders the fledgling company scrambled to fulfill. The entire project took Suzy and her early team two weeks to script, cast, build sets, and film together with an agency partner. The video concludes its romp through everyday odor issues with our porcelain princess's blend of humor and whimsy—a tone of voice that's become characteristic of the entire brand.

"So whether you need to pinch a loaf at work, cut a rope at a party, or lay a brick at your boyfriend's, your days of embarrassing smells or prairie-dogging it are over. Poo-Pourri: Our business is to make it smell like your business never even happened!"

Over the last decade, thanks to this video and dozens

of hilarious and witty marketing campaigns like it, Poo-Pourri has generated more than $300 million in total sales. And while Suzy embraces the humor in what she does, she's dead serious about relying more on curiosity and intuition than best practices in order to do her best work.

"We don't trust ourselves," she said. "We've been taught to trust experts. It's a social conditioning. We have to de-program ourselves out of that."

Suzy learned this lesson the hard way. Before starting Poo-Pourri, she tried to launch multiple companies in her twenties, mainly brick-and-mortar businesses like tanning salons and beauty parlors. Each time, the business failed. Twice, Suzy had to file for bankruptcy, and in the 2008 financial crisis, she lost everything. Her cars and her home were repossessed, her savings were depleted, and her business closed its doors for good. To make matters worse, throughout that difficult professional time, she was also struggling through an abusive marriage—one she later left. Today, she views all of it as her preparation to launch Poo-Pourri.

"I know shit. Literally, shit in my life." And given her past failures, Suzy vowed never to launch another company again. "I had sworn off business. I had deemed myself the worst entrepreneur in the world. I was like, 'That's it. I'm done.'"

Then one fateful day, her curiosity caused her to question everything she knew. Suzy's brother-in-law had just emerged from the bathroom at his house, where he was hosting a party, and he turned to Suzy to complain about the odor. "Why can't anybody figure out how to get rid of it once and for all?" he asked.

Suzy couldn't shake it. It seemed so simple. So many companies sell products to solve this, but all they seem to do is combine a good smell with the bad one, which just creates a new kind of bad one. Suddenly, she realized the real problem. "Once the odor is created, it goes out into the air," she said. "So I was curious to figure out if we could address the problem before it starts."

Could you trap the odor inside the water before it had the chance to escape in the first place?

Suzy wasn't a scientist. She'd never been hired to develop new products for Procter & Gamble. But despite that lack of expertise (or perhaps because of it), her intuition led her straight to a powerful insight. A simple but foundational question sparked Suzy's curiosity: what if you could trap the odor underwater?

"I was obsessed," she said. "I went inside."

Unlike her previous businesses, where she was motivated by external validation like money or recognition, she allowed her curiosity to consume her with this new problem. She focused on answering each question that arose en route to creating Poo-Pourri, investigating the world around her with every step she took.

Q: Why hadn't anybody solved this problem?

A: They were addressing the problem after it was too late.

Q: How can we address the problem before it arises?

A: Well, to do that, we'd need something that can let solids into the water but prevent gasses from escaping—like oils! Luckily for Suzy, in her past companies and in her personal life, she'd become obsessed with the use of natural essential oils in various beauty products.

Q: What if we could use those sweet-smelling products to trap gasses underneath the water?

A: No luck. The oils simply bead up into little balls when they sit on water or when they're disturbed by solids breaking through them.

Q: Can we get the oil to lay down across the top of the water instead?

Suzy didn't know the answer, but she was hell-bent on figuring it out. Purchasing a few basic ingredients, she mixed and matched various substances in her home and, after nine months of testing, found the right combination to solve that problem. A few sprays of this new oil mixture, now with Suzy's secret ingredients, causes a film to form along the top of the water, trapping odors inside.

It took nine more months after creating the product to figure out how to package it. Suzy was familiar with building businesses, but she'd never worked in consumer packaged goods before. So she scheduled coffee meetings with manufacturers and marketers in that space to find the right partners. Sometimes, she'd be encouraged by those who might say something like, "I love what you're doing, and I can introduce you to someone who can help you." Other times, a negative response or a dead-end would be a valuable reminder that she needed to revisit her plan. Rather than get discouraged, her curiosity drove her forward. She was grateful for the chance to improve her thinking and course-correct with each step she took. She preferred to be vaguely right rather than precisely wrong.

"All of it was just about curiosity and a challenge," she said. But her biggest challenge yet would be the marketing. How do you educate consumers about a product they don't know how to use, to solve a problem they don't want to discuss?

"No one wanted to talk about this subject matter. So I knew it had to be funny because that helped break the ice from this taboo topic, and I knew it had to be pretty because I was tired of the aluminum cans."

You know the type. You trace your eyes around a meticulously decorated bathroom only to land on a tin can wrapped in stock imagery of clouds and flowers. "I loved the juxtaposition of [Poo-Pourri] looking like a perfume bottle when it's actually a poop spray."

To get the full experience, I ordered myself some Poo-Pourri. (To my wife: you're welcome.)

The product arrived in a sleek black box with two bottles carefully nestled in some shredded black paper. This particular product is called "Smoky Woods," though it's more sweet-smelling than smoky. The spray is packaged in a palm-sized spritz bottle, the kind of upright container with sloping shoulders that reminded me of my mom's perfume when I was a kid.

Across the front of the bottle is a white sash reading "POO-POURRI." The background design makes it feel like you're looking at a hidden garden, maybe in Camelot or ancient Greece, with twisting vines dotted with golden leaves. If you look closely enough, there are a few water pipes running behind the vines while two white cherubs sit on opposite corners. One is playing the trumpet, the other tossing some toilet paper across the top of the bottle. On the side of the bottle, there's a limerick:

"There once was a young lad from Rhone, whose odor he'd rather disown. Now he's taming his poo, by anointing the loo, and now happily sits on his throne."

In all of this, one thing became clear: Poo-Pourri has meticulously combined humor and elegance to create a product that's easy to like. (As for my actual use of the product, let's just pretend my editor removed all the smelly details that I was definitely *not* too embarrassed to write about. Yep. That's what happened. Totally.)

With a final product wrapped in humor and elegance, Suzy had completed the final step in launching a business. But that was never actually part of her plan. "I never actually thought about bringing this to market. Remember, I had sworn off being in business altogether. It was more that I was looking at the challenge and wondering, 'Can I invent this? Can I stop odor?'"

Suzy's undying curiosity led her to pursue this path. She let the desire to find her own answers carry her forward, acting like an investigator into her environment rather than an expert who possesses all the answers. Quite frankly, Suzy didn't have all the answers, and she thinks this might actually be a strength instead of a liability in our work.

"What you don't know is actually your superpower, so use your ignorance to your advantage."

That's the difference between the average individual at work and those who trust their intuition. The latter seems to be endlessly curious, never satisfied with answers like, "Because that's the best practice" or "That's how we do things around here."

"When you and an inspired idea are dancing together, you don't have to know anything," Suzy said. "It's like there is no big plan. It's more like, 'Oh my gosh, let's go this direction—yeah, that looks really good!' And if it doesn't work, I'd go, 'Oh, what about this direction?'"

> **"What you don't know is actually your superpower, so use your ignorance to your advantage."**
>
> **–Poo-Pourri CEO Suzy Batiz**

It's easy to hear the stories in this book and simply think, "Easy for them to say. They don't work in *my* office, with *my* team, with *my* boss, inside *my* industry, with *my* budget. It's easy for them to spark *their* curiosity." I get it. But I'd encourage you to rely on two things in your work to get inspired and begin to trust your intuition over best practices: anger and audacity.

Get angry at average work. Then have the audacity to do something exceptional. Too often, we stop at the anger. We get frustrated with our work, and we point to reasons why we're stuck. We don't have any answers that sound pithier or cleaner or more practical than the best practice, so we just follow that. In these instances, we are too focused on having the right answer. However, to consider or contemplate the world around us (intuition), we don't actually *need* the right answer. Instead, we need the right questions. Constant curiosity drives us forward in better ways than merely following a list of instructions handed to us.

"You can get advice all you want," Suzy said, "But then you need to pull back into yourself to see how that feels. You are the creator. You are the one who has the power in this situation. Remember that."

In the business world, too many of us actively remove curiosity from the process. In our efforts to mitigate risk or justify our actions, we try to gather all the information we need ahead of time to say with confidence, "This is the right path forward." It's almost like curiosity is dangerous. Because any moment where we begin to ask questions implies we don't have all the answers.

We need to flip this on its head. Rather than gather up all the answers we think we need to justify acting, we need to act to find our answers. Not only does this trigger our curiosity and begin our process of using our intuition, but it's also more logical. Knowing what works ahead of time implies that every situation is identical. Instead, that upfront knowledge is merely an approximation—a generality that we must make specific at some point. I say, start with the specific situation we face first. It's there we'll find better answers.

"We fall into analysis paralysis," Suzy said. "Instead, keep going toward your idea. Keep moving. Movement is the key, especially inspired movement. Start noticing things, and when you get a no, don't go in that direction. But keep moving."

That spark of curiosity got Suzy going, but really, her career has been about constant movement forward. She asks questions, investigates, and learns. Repeat that process. Forever. There are no final answers, no final state of "knowing" what works—only the constant honing of your intuition to consider details around you as they change.

"I've never had that *aha, I've made it* moment. I still don't have that feeling," she said. "I'm not interested in that end point. I'm just curious the whole way."

In reality, constant movement forward is all a career really is. What if we cared less about finishing and more about moving? What if we cared less about being experts and cared more about being investigators?

COMBATTING CRAP WITH CONSTANT CURIOSITY

When I worked in ad sales early on in my career at Google, I was so confused by how advertisers made decisions. They spent millions of dollars with Google over our competitors based on projections rather than tests. I'd walk into an office at twenty-four, put up a bunch of data generated by our internal business intelligence team claiming that, sure, we can guarantee a certain number of impressions and clicks for your ads. But we couldn't possibly *know* that! Nothing had actually been created yet; nothing had been launched into the world. There had been no movement forward. We were making decisions based solely on theory.

I remember thinking, "I have no idea if you'll see these results. If you're so curious, why don't you test something?" I couldn't hand them the answer, but I could definitely tell them how to go find it. Unfortunately, instead of trying the latter, they asked for the former.

It's not just in advertising. This is everywhere in business. We agonize over the exact steps we need to take to get promoted or grow our social media following. We download blueprints and step-by-step guides. All of this stuff seems relevant in theory, but how do we know any of it will work in reality?

Whether we're marketers developing new content, sales leaders documenting a new process, or product designers crafting the user experience, we seem to squash our curiosity and ignore our intuition. It's like we actually want to be average. But I know you don't. So let's act accordingly.

"People don't share good. They share great," Suzy said. "And everything can be great, but you have to keep tweaking it until you've refined it."

To illustrate this, Suzy pointed to how Poo-Pourri creates videos. For each ad, they shoot multiple intros and multiple conclusions. Then they put all the various combinations online to test the outcomes. "What we're looking for is that scenario where it's not just a good video, it's an epic video." How do you create a good video? Endless experts can tell you. How do you create an epic video? You have to go figure that out for yourself.

It's been a decade since Suzy identified the root of a rather smelly problem, and she's just as curious today. As the CEO (sorry, PEO) of a thriving business, her job is not only to pursue her own curiosity but to spark the same urge in her team. This only gets harder as a company scales.

"A cell is either in a growth phase or a protection phase," she said. "What's a startup? It's growing. What's a large corporation? It's in protection phase."

To push her team to stay curious and create better work, Suzy divided the company into halves. She has a "protective" part of the business called operations. Their job is to execute on established processes. They maintain a status quo because their status quo is generating results. However, she knows this part of the business needs constant updating. The "status quo" must always change and improve. In order to achieve that, Suzy relies on the creative half.

By working in tandem, the two sides of the business avoid complacency and conventional wisdom. The creative side hunts for what could be new or next or better, and the protective side must then update based on what their peers learn. Like Suzy, the team conducts their work using an endless process of curiosity. They never settle for anything resembling "the playbook." Once something begins to feel rote, the creative side looks for ways to push it forward.

"We need more makers in the world," Suzy said. "We

need more people following inspired ideas, and we need more people not doing it the way it's always been done, because the way it's always been done is not working."

THE INSTANT CLARITY GENERATOR

Gary Klein's research into intuition suggests that it's our ability to arrive at an answer quicker, but I think his contemporary Gerd Gigerenzer has a slightly more nuanced interpretation. His research suggests that intuition is our ability to identify the pathway *toward* a conclusion, not the conclusion itself. In other words, we're able to quickly and intuitively identify which information is useful and which is irrelevant—a profoundly useful skill in the era of Advice Overload.

As Gigerenzer said in an interview about his book *Gut Feelings: The Intelligence of the Unconscious*, "Gut instincts often rely on simple cues in the environment. In most situations, when people use their instincts, they are heeding these cues and ignoring other unnecessary information."

The German social psychologist is the director of the Max Planck Institute for Human Development in Berlin. He's primarily known by his peers for his research into the nature of intuitive thinking. His work suggests that we can use intuition to draw conclusions about various inputs, which then makes the right decision seem more obvious. Honing and trusting our intuition thus improves our decision-making process by informing all our decisions with the most relevant possible information. Rather than rely on what works in general, we can quickly identify the information that is most relevant to us. This is the exact skill we need to supplement or outright replace our reliance on best practices.

Think of it like going to the eye doctor and being shown different lenses. "Number one or number two? Number three or number four?" Your intuition helps you quickly hold up a possibility—an idea, an answer, a bit of advice—and quickly see which makes sense for you. Which helps you see things most clearly? Which fits best in your unique situation? Intuition is like an instant clarity generator after all.

Still, it can be hard to trust what we see, even if we see it clearly. We've suffered from learned helplessness for so long and have spent so much time believing that the best answers in our careers were hidden away in the minds of experts. This can make it difficult to actually implement what we see into our work. However, Gigerenzer's research suggests we should trust ourselves more, or as he says, it's often best to "go with what you know." In one of his most famous studies, he explored "the recognition heuristic."

In the study, Gigerenzer examined the decision-making

process of people who invest in the stock market. He observed that amateur investors typically pick companies they've heard about before—the recognition heuristic at work. But is that effective? To figure that out, Gigerenzer's team surveyed 360 people in Chicago and Munich. They asked these people to create a list of the best-known public companies in both areas. Then the research team created theoretical investment portfolios based on those responses. After six months of tracking their fake investment portfolio, the team found that their theoretical investments gained more value than the Dow and DAX markets, as well as some big-name mutual funds.

Gigerenzer began this exercise in the 1990s, and since then, his team has shown that companies selected at random by uninformed or "ordinary" investors consistently outperformed the predictions of well-informed, professional investors. Ignorance might be bliss, but ignorance of *best practices* is money.

As with many scientific studies, especially those focused on concepts like intuition, Gigerenzer's work doesn't definitely prove anything one way or another. However, it suggests something powerful: focusing on what we know and what we find for ourselves might lead to better ideas and answers.

To paraphrase Gigerenzer, it's impossible to know all of

the variables prior to making a decision, and not all the information from your past is relevant to your future. As a result, I think best practices become incredibly dangerous because of how precise and prescriptive they are. They seem so specific, but in reality, they lack the context that only you can provide. However, when we begin to deploy our intuition, we start considering the variables that best practices miss. We can't know them all, but we can come a lot closer than industry-wide generalities.

If every decision we make is "close enough," then our intuition ensures we're "as close as possible." In trying to escape the messiness of so many unknown variables in our work, we trust best practices. But Gigerenzer sees this as a mistake. He says that a well-honed intuition is our inherent ability to focus on the most important information—not the most commonly used or the trendiest—in order to make better decisions. In the end, that's the power of intuition. It's an instant clarity generator, and clarity comes from having the most relevant information possible. Not for others. Not in general. Not on average. For *us*.

That's how we can break this wheel: by asking the right questions.

So what questions can you ask? There are two different types: trigger questions and confirmation questions.

What should you question? Your context. As we'll explore in the coming chapters, your context is the combination of three different aspects of your work. To begin honing your intuition, you can ask one trigger question and one confirmation question about each aspect.

Together, these questions provide a process we can use to escape the endless cycle of best practices. Because screw the Muse and damn the best practices. By asking the right questions, we can unlock the power of our own intuition. We can make this skill concrete, accessible, and practical. We can escape the endless cycle of average work. Intuition is the sledgehammer we can use to break the wheel. Next, let's learn how to forge this powerful tool.

.

CHAPTER 4

INVESTIGATE YOURSELF

I grew up in Branford, Connecticut, a town of about 30,000 people, full of stereotypical suburban neighborhoods. As a kid, few activities were more exciting and nerve-wracking than riding the quads—the all-terrain vehicles owned by my friends Dan and Greg, brothers who lived down the street from me. Together with their younger brother Brandon, they'd periodically drive around the neighborhood, offering rides to only the V-est of VIPs. If you were lucky enough to get an invite, you'd amble aboard, cling to the brother driving the quad, and careen around the neighborhood, smiling like an idiot. It was the best of times. But occasionally, it was the worst of times.

Dan and Greg were way more confident than I was as

a kid. Greg, the oldest brother, was the consummate tinkerer, obsessed with tools and cars and engines. The quads were his ultimate plaything. Meanwhile, Dan was the daredevil child who loved speed and took risks. He'd do backflips into pools and leap off swing sets at the highest point. He acted like he was made of rubber. Then there was their bowl-cut-rocking, short-shorts-wearing, little dweeb of a friend tagging along—the same guy writing the words you're reading right now.

Every so often, Dan, Greg, and Brandon would take a group of boys from the neighborhood deep into the woods to a circular dirt track we called The Pits. This trail was full of sharp turns, unexpected branches jutting out, and a few boulders covered in dirt and moss. When we were around, the boulders became ramps—to the delight of three confident brothers and the horror of younger Jay.

Each and every time we'd ride quads around The Pits, Dan and Greg would ask if I wanted to drive one myself. Each and every time, I'd pretend I was super excited before finding a way to "settle" for riding on the back of theirs instead. (It's no wonder my sport of choice as a kid, basketball, forbids even the lightest tap on the arm.) Just the idea of hurtling at top speed toward a boulder made me want to hurl. So every single time, I refused to drive my own quad.

Except one time.

One time, I hemmed and hawed as usual. I gazed at my friends and saw they each expected me to decline. The internal agony felt too great, so I finally decided to try driving my own quad. Immediately, I felt more confident. More excited. More handsome. (Sure, why not?)

I grabbed a helmet and crammed it tightly onto my head. With total confidence, I selected my vehicle. Sure, I chose to drive the smallest quad typically reserved for Brandon, and sure, he was four or five years our junior, but that didn't matter. I was going to drive that quad.

I eased onto the cushion.

I gripped the handle.

I nodded toward my friends.

I stared at the track ahead.

I hit the gas!

And I...

...drove straight into a tree.

Yep.

But here's the weird part: I felt amazing. In fact, I'd never felt so successful in my life!

I'd gone maybe two miles-per-hour, drove for about three seconds, and needed the help of four friends (once they stopped laughing) to yank my vehicle back onto the track. But I felt victorious, like I could finally breathe after so much time spent suffocating over the decision.

I removed my helmet, brushed some leaves off my shirt, and Breakfast Clubbed my way out of there. *(Raises fist. Marches away triumphantly.)*

KNOWING VS. TRYING

Looking back, I can't believe I was afraid of anything. I think my brain had played a trick on me, convincing me that the goal was to *know* I'd succeed, rather than *try* to succeed. Make no mistake, the real goal is to try.

Instead, I wanted some absolute answers to my questions. *Would I be safe? Would I succeed? Would I look cool?* The gap between my status quo (refusing to drive) and what I imagined would make me feel awesome (whipping around the track like a pro) felt too great to cross without some predetermined answer, idea, or skill. It was crippling, like an immovable mental wall. But once I actually drove the quad, I felt awesome. I had clarity. I immediately crashed, which is the very definition of failure in this particular activity, yet I still felt successful. Why?

Because I tried.

I don't think any big mental barrier exists between our status quo and whatever we deem to be our best work. There is no thick, immovable wall. There's just a flimsy little screen between not trying and trying. There's just an inch between watching minnows float by your nose and snapping up a delicious meal. My issue was that I'd never even tried.

We do this at work all the time. We get stuck in the land of theory rather than trying to learn and discover new information in the real world. But I get it. The stakes are higher at work than when you're a kid driving ATVs with your friends. (Little Jay would not agree, but stay with me.) At work, we retreat into the safety of conventional wisdom or trendy new tactics because we can tell our bosses, clients, peers, or even ourselves the same thing: "We have the information we need to justify acting. Now we will act." Instead, when we rely on that spark of our curiosity, we are telling the world and ourselves, "I don't know the answers, but I'm still going to act." To paraphrase researcher and bestselling author Brené Brown, there is no creativity without vulnerability.

This is the power of what I call "trigger questions." They make it easier to become vulnerable. It's a way to spark curiosity in a way that feels concrete—as concrete as all those best practices that previously felt like the safer bet. Trigger questions can't be answered using industry expertise. Instead, they require self-awareness and situational awareness. When we ask a trigger question, we begin to act more like investigators than experts.

As a child, if I'd only made the goal *trying* instead of *succeeding*, I might have succeeded sooner. I thought I needed some theoretical answer: a lengthy explanation from Dan or Greg to coach me, an ego boost from a pretty girl walking by the track, or maybe some dope new gear that would help me Evel Knievel my way around The Pits. Because of this need to have the perfect situation, I never acted.

To do our best in anything, we have to want to know what will happen in reality, not in theory. If we could spark our curiosity in an on-demand way, like a switch we can flip during uninspired or confusing moments, maybe we'd make decisions that are better than any best practice.

Similarly, the only way to break free from the wheel of average work is to try. The difference between glomming onto a trend and thinking for yourself is the simple act of asking a trigger question. Once we begin thinking for ourselves, we see the wheel of best practices for what it is: insufficient information. Next, we can busy ourselves with finding the best possible answers using the details of our context.

This is the power of a trigger question—an open-ended question about your specific situation that can only be answered through reflection and testing. The words "your" and "we" and "our" appear in these questions. They force us to investigate our environment to find the best answer for a given situation. Since our path might seem unconventional, once we answer a trigger question, we can then ask the second type to ensure we're thinking clearly: confirmation questions.

If trigger questions spark your curiosity and prompt investigation, then confirmation questions reflect back on your sleuthing. Are you on the right track? Are you thinking clearly? Is this really the proper approach for you? What did you learn, and how does that change how you move forward? We can only answer confirmation questions using firsthand learning or results. Taken together, trigger questions and confirmation questions help us make decisions based on whatever works for us, regardless of the convention.

After several years of developing hundreds of stories of exceptional, often unconventional people for my podcast, I've pulled out six specific questions: three trigger questions and three confirmation questions. These questions come in pairs, with a confirmation question helping you reaffirm your answer from the corresponding trigger question.

TRIGGER QUESTION	CONFIRMATION QUESTION
Spark your curiosity to begin your investigation.	Identify clues to ensure you're on the right path.
1) Trigger Question 1	2) Confirmation Question 1
3) Trigger Question 2	4) Confirmation Question 2
5) Trigger Question 3	6) Confirmation Question 3

As for what you should ask questions *about*, that much should be clear by now: your context. Your specific situation holds all kinds of variables that no best practice takes into account. If the best practices do take them into account, consider it a happy accident. So let's stop relying on happy accidents. Let's stop hoping that best practices deliver us to our best work and start proactively getting there ourselves.

Your context is comprised of three parts: you, your audience, and your resources. If we ask the right questions about these three elements, then we can begin to wield our intuition like a sledgehammer against the wheel of average work.

PIECE OF YOUR CONTEXT	TRIGGER QUESTION	CONFIRMATION QUESTION
You The person or people doing the work.	*(Explored This Chapter)*	*(Explored This Chapter)*
Your Audience The person or people receiving the work.	*(Chapter 5)*	*(Chapter 5)*
Your Resources The means to make the work happen.	*(Chapter 6)*	*(Chapter 6)*

THE HOT DOG, THE PRESIDENT, AND YOU

Let's start with questions about you. Imagine you are
Lisa Schneider. She's the chief digital officer at Merriam-
Webster Dictionary, and it's her unenviable job to make
the dictionary seem cool in the digital age. (That's kind
of like teaching Grandma how to twerk...but hey, that's
the job.)

Just for a moment, think about your favorite dictionary. .
Can you picture it? What's the brand on the cover? Is there
even a cover in your mind? Are you able to picture a book
at all? If you're like me, your relationship with the dic-

tionary is rather void of any branding whatsoever: just a simple Google search for the word in question.

Dictionaries are boring commodities. One article in The Guardian describes dictionaries as "serious, sober documents, with little room for excitement." The article explains how even an eighteenth-century lexicographer (dictionary editor) named Nathaniel Bailey got so bored creating definitions that he simply called a spider "an insect well known" and a cherry "a fruit well known." So unless the lexicographer gives up on life like Bailey apparently had, a word's definition is set, with little room for creativity or differentiation between competitors. As a result, if you're in Lisa Schneider's shoes, the odds are already stacked against you as a marketing leader. The company's marketing approach wasn't helping either.

"I came into the job [in August 2014] and was having a great time, but then I looked at our social media feeds, and they were bland and pre-programmed and not at all interactive," she said. "There was this huge disconnect."

Every day on Twitter, the marketing team shared the same boring things: a word of the day in the morning and a quiz to test your knowledge of definitions at night. Every. Single. Stinking. Day.

"When I tell people I work for the dictionary, unanimously,

the first thing that they say is, 'Oh my gosh, that's so cool,'"
Lisa told me. So why did their marketing feel anything
but? Before we understand the problem, we first have to
understand the goal of a lexicographer, and more specifically, we have to debunk a common misconception.

Contrary to popular belief, lexicographers don't actually
create any sacred rules that govern language. That rigid-
ness you might be thinking of belongs more to a grammar
stickler than a lexicographer. In reality, lexicographers
study language as it's actually spoken, documenting its
evolution in the dictionary.

"We call ourselves descriptive, not prescriptive," Lisa said.
"It's not our jobs to sit up there in an ivory tower and tell
people what words should mean. We catalog language
as it is used."

Unfortunately, the brand's plodding and predictable
approach to social media simply didn't capture what it
really means to work at the dictionary. In order to follow
and document language changes, the team has to be very
engaged and excited by popular culture. They also have
to remain flexible to constantly changing the rules. None
of that was evident in their marketing.

"People might assume that the dictionary is a dusty book
on the shelf and a bunch of stuffy people defending lan-

guage as it should be, but the truth is really the opposite," Lisa said. She describes her team as "warm, witty, and wonderful." (Look, she works for the dictionary. She likes alliteration.) Every day, she would show up to work and start "laughing and learning." (Again: dictionary.) However, none of that emotion was coming through in the way they communicated with the public. So after two years on the job, Lisa decided enough was enough.

"Let's show the world how fun and relevant we really are," she told her team.

This is a great example of an aspirational anchor. An aspirational anchor is a simple declaration of how you'll make a difference in your life or the lives of others. Just to clarify again, this is your intent to make a *difference*, not a *profit*. Aspirational anchors turn your vague desire to be exceptional into something specific and concrete. Like Mike Brown declaring, "I'll create the world's strongest coffee," Lisa urged her team to gaze beyond conventional norms and aspire to do something great: become just as warm, witty, and wonderful in their marketing as they are as people.

Unlike the team at Merriam-Webster, most of us never anchor to anything aspirational enough in our work. For example, if you were in Lisa's situation and wanted to improve the company's Twitter account, what would you normally do? Maybe you'd think, "Let's grow our Twitter followers by 50 percent." But you're not inspiring anyone. Quantitative validation is how you measure the achievement of an aspiration, not articulate the aspiration itself. Other times, rather than focusing on a metric, perhaps you'd say, "Let's go viral!" (Oh my gosh, are people still thinking this? It's 2018! Hashtag *no*. Stop that. You stop that right now.)

Rather than fall victim to the average thinking of her space, Lisa elevated the gaze of her entire team with her aspirational anchor: let's show the world how fun and relevant we really are.

"I can't tell you why they were posting a word of the day in the morning and a call-to-action to play a game in the afternoon and nothing else," Lisa said. "You know, it's called social media. You can talk to people!"

There was none of that sociability or tone of voice that she heard all around the office. "I can't tell you why. I can only tell you that there was this huge gap, and we were missing out on an amazing opportunity to show everybody how cool we really are."

One of their first steps toward achieving their aspirational anchor was the creation of "emoji threads"—playful tweets that explain homophones. Merriam-Webster defines a homophone as "one of two or more words pronounced alike but different in meaning or derivation or spelling (such as the words *to, too,* and *two*)." So, for instance, the words *peak, peek,* and *pique* would be shared together in one tweet, with a short definition and single emoji next to each of them. Next to *peak* (the pointed top of a mountain) would be a mountain icon; next to *peek* (a brief or furtive look), a couple eyeballs glancing to the left; and next to *pique* (a transient feeling of wounded vanity), a yellow face, eyebrows furrowed, snorting air out of its nose—the emoji version of *harrumph!*

Over the next few weeks, Lisa saw an uptick in both retweets and delighted comments from followers—just a few dozen, but packed with enough emotion that she decided to lean into the approach. She moved quickly to hire the company's first full-time social media manager. Appropriately, their new teammate, a former English teacher named Lauren Naturale, found the job posting through a link Merriam-Webster tweeted. Lauren would help Lisa build on the success of emoji threads and, more importantly, infuse everything the brand shared on social media with the same tone of voice.

One of their earliest successes happened the Friday before Memorial Day 2016. As that weekend approached, the team was debating a crucial question that needed to be answered before the holiday: *is the hot dog a sandwich?* (See? Crucial!)

Noticing the passion and hilarity of this internal debate, Lisa and Lauren agreed that Merriam-Webster should write a blog post on the matter. On the Friday before the weekend, the brand tweeted their final opinion: "Have a great #MemorialDayWeekend. The hot dog is a sandwich."

They justified their stance online by writing, "We know: the idea that a hot dog is a sandwich is heresy to some of you. But given that the definition of sandwich is 'two or more slices of bread or a split roll having a filling in between,' there is no sensible way around it. If you want a meatball sandwich on a split roll to be a kind of sandwich, then you have to accept that a hot dog is also a kind of sandwich."

So said the dictionary. And the internet, naturally, lost its freaking mind.

"I trusted you!" tweeted one unsatisfied follower.

"You've gone too far!" declared another.

The brand took a stance, and these people were taking a stance right back. One woman even poured out her soul on Twitter, doing her best Shakespeare impression when she wrote, "And yea, the hot dog is NOT a sandwich, for the meat tis exposed to the heavens and not blanketed by bread! This is my decree."

Lisa was shocked by the passionate response to their simple tweet. "Oh my God, I did *not* know people had such strong and deeply held convictions about whether or not the hot dog is a sandwich! This was a Thing with a capital T. This was our first big thing."

The brand even received press coverage from the tweet. From Fox News to *USA Today* to the *Today Show* to food blogs like Eater, Merriam-Webster was suddenly part of the conversation in a way they hadn't been in...maybe ever.

"You have to know what your power is. For us, the power is connecting language to people's everyday." Their aspirational anchor had unleashed that power. Sometimes the team at Merriam-Webster simply added more of their sassy-but-smart commentary to what they'd previously been sharing.

Rather than tweet a straightforward article titled "Is it 'Damp Down' or 'Tamp Down'?" they'd share an image of a grumpy looking cat in a bathtub and write a new thought above the link, saying, "Does 'damp down' drive you up the wall? What about 'tamp down'? Either way, let's take it down a notch." Other times, they'd find ways to participate in new pop culture discussions. "Current research shows use of 'ginormous' as early as 1942," they said in response to a trivia question from the mobile game show HQ Trivia. "Moral of the story: if you want to win at HQ, read our site a bunch?"

The more Merriam-Webster acted and sounded like this, the more their results grew. Merriam-Webster now has over 720,000 followers on Twitter alone. They've also grown their Instagram audience from a few thousand to 57,000 in just under two years. In 2016, the year Lisa first articulated her aspirational anchor, Twitter followers grew by 456 percent, views of their content increased by more than 6,000 percent, and their press mentions jumped by 7,000 percent—because who the heck was writing about a dictionary in the press before then? Today, it seems that everyone is telling Merriam-Webster's story.

"Move Over, Wikipedia. Dictionaries Are Hot Again," wrote Katherine Rosman of *The New York Times*. In the article, Rosman lauds tweets from Merriam-Webster during the 2016 presidential election season. On the brand's Twitter account, the team had started sharing what they called "trending lookups," or words that were experiencing sudden increases in searches on their site. Due to the truly insane nature of the 2016 campaign between Donald Trump and Hillary Clinton, words like "fascism" and "demagogue" and, quite memorably, "deplorable" all saw sharp spikes in lookups. By doing what they do best (observing and documenting language change) and adding their natural tone of voice, Merriam-Webster became a prominent part of the cultural conversation. The press hits just kept coming.

TIME published the article "18 Times Merriam-Webster Was a Political Troll," while BuzzFeed released a series of articles covering the dictionary's smartest-friend-at-the-bar tone on Twitter. Both *The Washington Post* and, returning for more, *The New York Times* told the story behind Lisa and Lauren's work as others rushed to cover the internet sensation that was Merriam-Webster Dictionary. Coverage included Slate, *NPR*, Mic, Vox, Vice, CollegeHumor, The Hill, Huffington Post, *NBC News*, *The Independent*...even *Vogue*. That's right. *Vogue*.

You might even say that the dictionary is now (pause for effect) "in" vogue.

(I mean, you might say that. I wouldn't. That's too punny. But someone might.)

"Very quickly, and I hate this word, it did start becoming viral," Lisa admitted. "We haven't spent any money. It's been totally organic." Finally, after years of feeling like a dusty old book on a digital shelf, the brand was part of the daily conversation on social media feeds across the world. It all began with articulating their aspirational anchor.

It's here that we find ourselves with the first trigger question, the first question we can use to understand the first part of our context—ourselves.

So ask yourself, **what is your aspirational anchor?**

Aspirational anchors combine two powerful things in our work: our intent for the future, and some kind of hunger we have today to rise above the status quo. Most people understand some version of their intent for the future. For example, Lisa knew right away she wanted Merriam-Webster's brand to be part of the conversation in a way they hadn't been before. But it's the hunger she identified in herself and her team that made her anchor aspirational enough to achieve something great. She admitted out loud that their brand's voice was too bland.

Intent + Hunger = Aspirational Anchor

If you can anchor to the right aspiration, then you create

a filter for vetting ideas and advice quicker. Aspirational anchors provide each of us with a first line of defense against Advice Overload. Sometimes, a best practice makes it all the way through the filter. If you recall Mike Brown from Death Wish Coffee, his anchor was to create the world's strongest coffee. Therefore, it made sense to listen to experts who advised him to narrow his product line. On the other hand, it didn't make sense to roast the more common arabica coffee bean, given that robusta retains more caffeine when roasted. Likewise, for Lisa and her team, they could easily decide which marketing trends made sense to use and to what degree.

Oftentimes on Twitter, marketers will find a few types of tweets that work, then fall back on them repeatedly—the path to what Lisa called "bland, predictable, and staid" sharing. Instead of merely glomming onto the trend of social media automation, Merriam-Webster decided to hire a social media manager to respond right away and publish more newsworthy content. Why? To show the world they are fun and relevant.

To confirm that your aspirational anchor is on the right path toward success, we can ask our first confirmation question: **What is your unfair advantage?** In other words, why you? Lisa Schneider had experienced her team's daily warmth and wit, and she realized just how rare and welcome that would be on social media. Like

Lisa, we can all spend more time contemplating the unique experiences, abilities, and traits that we and those we work with possess. What is it about you or your team that will enable you to reach your aspiration? As personal statements, aspirational anchors should give you a reason to apply who you are to your work. Who you are is the one thing nobody else can access. It's your unfair advantage. Are you using that advantage to its full extent in your work?

Entrepreneur and creative director Doug Kessler has been thinking about this for years.

BRINGING YOUR FULL SELF TO WORK

"If you actually bring your full self and you sit in front of whatever it is you're doing, you'll find you've got a lot more to bring to it," said Kessler, the cofounder of B2B content marketing agency Velocity Partners.

Few marketers challenge conventional wisdom more frequently than Kessler. The prolific blogger and speaker has a reputation for putting his finger on whatever is broken in the marketing industry. And once he does, he presses it. Hard. The project that made him famous among marketers across the globe was the 2013 slideshow, "Crap. The Content Marketing Deluge." In this piece, he definitely brings his full self to the work, making a smart, sarcastic, and impassioned plea to the marketing industry to avoid publishing more crappy content. Five years after publishing it, "Crap" has more than 4.7 million views.

"Maybe not teenage-YouTube-narcissist viral," Kessler wrote in a blog post in 2018, "but as close to B2B viral as we expect to get." Even in casual asides in his writing, he is clearly present in his work.

Kessler believes there is a practical reason why we should insert who we are into our work. Because doing so leads to the best outcomes. "This is very much a results-driven thing," he said. "We know we're going to work better if we find that zone where we enjoy what we're doing. There's a very hard-nosed rationale for the stuff we're talking about here even though it sounds touchy-feely to some people in the business world."

As a longtime content marketer myself, I know just how easy it can be to disassociate ourselves from people we admire—in my case, people like Doug Kessler. Sometimes, we don't feel we're in control of our decisions like others who succeed. We might say, "That's nice in theory, Dougie-boy, but I'm not a cofounder of my company like you." Other times, we might envy certain personality traits that we lack: the wit, the wisdom, the charm (you're welcome, Doug). We think, "Well, that's not me." But the point isn't to be the people we admire. The point is to possess the same level of self-awareness.

A perfect example of this behavior is Scott Stratten. Scott is a keynote speaker and business author, and few people seem to bring their full selves to their work quite like him. He rants on his show the *UnPodcast*, which he refers to as "the business podcast for the fed-up." He tells beautiful human stories in his bestselling books like *UnMarketing*, *UnSelling*, and *UnBranding*.

As a professional speaker, Scott only delivers keynote speeches, meaning he addresses the entire audience all at once, sharing a big idea or eagle-eye view of the industry in his talks. Or should I say, his yells?

"What we mean when we say 'millennials' are people who are younger than us, and we don't like you!" he shouted from stage to raucous laughter. "Millennials don't like meetings. I just read that this week. 'Millennials don't like meetings.' *Who the hell likes meetings?!* What is the demographic that goes, 'Meeting? Giddyup! Let's go, I gotta be in there!'"

It's clear that Scott brings his full self to his work. That's a big part of his aspirational anchor. "I want to be as authentically me on stage as I can be."

Since he was twelve years old, Scott aspired to be a professional speaker. It was then, in his home outside Toronto, that he first remembered seeing motivational speaker Les Brown on TV as part of a pledge drive.

"I sat on the floor and just watched him, and I vividly remember thinking, 'You can do *that* for a living?' And I knew from that day forward I was going to be a speaker."

After working in HR to start his career, then running an agency specializing in creating viral videos for brands, Scott decided to make speaking his full-time role in 2010. By 2016, he was booking $1 million in speaking fees per year. But no matter where he speaks or who is in the audience, he understands the power of bringing his full self—not as some lofty ideal but as a practical way to deliver the best possible speech. The more he understands who he is and how his personality lends itself to a better talk, the more he becomes an exception from the average speakers out there.

So what's Scott's unfair advantage? Where do I even begin? How about on the top of his head, since his hair is the very first thing you notice. You see, Scott Stratten, professional business keynote speaker, sports a man bun.

"I just want to cover something right now," Scott begins in every speech. "Should I address the man bun now...or after the talk?"

The man bun is just the hairy cherry on top of a particular style that makes Scott look like Scott—and no one else. For each of his more than sixty keynote speeches per year, he waltzes onto stages sporting a big, bushy beard to match his bun up top, along with a black polo shirt, jeans, and work boots. As he waves his arms, you also notice the tattoos on his forearms, like the one reading "UNLEARN" in black letters, a nod to Scott's belief that we should unlearn hatred and prejudice and treat each other with respect. Scott looks more like a blacksmith or a biker who only recently left the gang for a more civilized life. Whatever your interpretation, he simply doesn't look like the average business speaker. He's an exception to the norm.

Not everyone appreciates that.

"I was giving a talk in Vegas, and it was my first really big talk," Scott recalled. He'd been hired to deliver a speech to 1,500 insurance agents at eight in the morning, a brutal time for a speech in any city, let alone Las Vegas. "This was during March Madness, so they had a tailgate party the night before, with a literal truck tailgate in the ballroom. And an open bar."

The morning of his speech, Scott sauntered down from his hotel room to the conference center with his usual look: the beard, the bun, the black shirt, jeans, and boots.

Before he could enter the room, he was approached by a woman in a headset who was coordinating part of the event.

"She came up to me and gave me the once over and goes, 'Can you go change into something more appropriate?'"

Scott scanned the room and noticed a man in a suit on stage delivering the opening preamble before his keynote. He looked like the stereotypical business speaker, the kind this woman wanted Scott to look like too, and he was bombing. The attendees felt lifeless. All energy had been sucked out of the room.

Scott looked up at him and back at the woman in the headset. "I promise you," he said, "when I'm done, nobody is going to walk out and say, 'That was awesome, but I wish he had on a tie.'"

"Whatever," the woman grunted, and she walked away.

As the struggling insurance expert finished his brief talk, Scott greeted him stage-side, where the man promptly handed him his microphone. ("He thought I was the sound guy.") Scott smiled, knowing full well what was about to happen. He pinned the microphone onto his shirt, waited for his introduction, and strode onto the stage.

"I could feel the room going, what the hell is this?" They couldn't figure out why the sound guy, or maybe a blacksmith, or maybe a biker entering the next phase of his career was about to speak to them. Surely, he wasn't a professional keynote speaker?

An hour later, all 1,500 insurance agents gave Scott a standing ovation. It was the only such ovation of the five-day event. As he walked off stage, he saw the woman in the headset again. "So," he said, handing her his microphone, "still think I needed the tie?"

That's how it so often goes for Scott Stratten, keynote speaker. He doesn't look anything like your average keynote speaker, because he's not trying to be an average speaker. He's trying to be exceptional, and in doing so, he knows he has to use what makes him an exception. He just wishes more speakers would do the same.

> **The point isn't to be the people we admire.
> The point is to possess the same
> level of self-awareness.**

"It's this epidemic in business, and it's not isolated to speaking. We all want the shortcut," he said. "My biggest beef is that [speakers] sell programs to people that use the word 'just,' and 'just' is the biggest red flag for any business or success program. You're 'just' missing this or 'just' do that. That doesn't exist. There is no 'just.'"

In reality, success is the byproduct of a combination of little things used together in our work. "But [speakers] can't package that," he said in disgust. "There's no course that sells effort. There's no course that sells the idea that it takes a hell of a lot of time, luck, timing, and skill. Because that doesn't sell."

Scott recalls attending an event for public speaking professionals. One of his peers was describing Scott's speaking style within earshot, after which the other person merely shrugged and said, "Well that's his *thing*."

While it is indeed his "thing," Scott points to the overly manicured, carefully crafted images of many professional speakers. He believes others will manufacture an image that isn't truly who they are in order to sell gigs. Scott doesn't believe in this approach. Instead, he tries to be himself on stage. He wears polo shirts because he waves his arms too much to wear more restrictive shirts or jackets. He chose black polos so audiences can't see just how sweaty he gets on stage. He wears boots because he's on his feet all day. As for the beard and man bun? His wife likes the way they look.

It's a subtle difference. Scott doesn't dress or act a certain way to sell something. Instead, the way Scott dresses and acts sells. He starts with being fully himself in his work, then he finds clients who want that.

"I talk about authenticity and talk about disruption. I don't know if I could talk about that in a strong way without being that myself."

As Scott shows, those who bring their full selves to their work often possess an advantage over the average work in their industry. We started investigating our specific context by asking a trigger question about ourselves: **what is my aspirational anchor?**

Next, we should ask the confirmation question: **what is my unfair advantage?** How are you uniquely qualified to achieve your aspiration?

THE MOST OVERLOOKED QUESTION

When I worked in venture capital, I noticed how investors would routinely ask startup founders this very same question. "What is your unfair advantage?" At Next-View Ventures, we invested in entrepreneurs more than products, and we knew that competitors would copy successful products dozens of times over. As a result, we wanted to understand what advantages a founder could use to outpace the competition.

I can't speak for my former colleagues or peers in VC, but I can tell you that it was, and still is, my fiercest belief that every individual and team had some unfair advantages. Therefore, rather than probing for whether an advantage *existed*, that confirmation question reveals whether the founder had taken the time to identify it. Identifying your unfair advantage separates the commodities from the exceptions. Venture capitalists prefer to invest in exceptions, and we should all prefer to act like them in order to do our best work.

Doug Kessler is exceptional because of his wit and wisdom. Scott Stratten is exceptional because of his ability to be himself and speak his mind with zero jargon. However, if we're going to be exceptional, we shouldn't just try to be like them. That's the downside of copying those we admire or hear about in books or blogs or podcasts. We try to force ourselves into someone else's mold. In reality, we shouldn't copy their traits—unless we're similarly witty, wise, sarcastic, and smart. No, the real trait we should copy from these two men is their willingness to identify and then deploy what makes them different than others in their work. What that means for you all depends on you or your team.

That's arguably the hardest answer to accept: "It depends." For instance, should you sound more sarcastic in your writing? It depends. What are you writing? Are you genuinely sarcastic as a person? Because of all the variables, it depends. Your specific answer also doesn't replace best practices as "the" answer.

For instance, upon creating the refreshing emoji-thread tweets, Merriam-Webster broke from their boring, predictable approach on Twitter—but if they then automated the emoji threads, is that any better than their previous obsession with a word of the day? I'd argue they'd be back where they started. No, it's not enough to simply *replace* existing best practices with new ones. We have to constantly question everything we put into practice in order to continually improve. That's why asking questions is so much more powerful than glomming onto previously accepted answers.

Merriam-Webster's team has become adept at this process. For example, once they identified that their tone of voice improved their content distribution efforts, they found ways to involve other brands with complementary voices. No partnership showcases this better than their collaboration with the Los Angeles County Museum of Art (LACMA). Together, they created a game called Words and Features on Twitter. LACMA would share the image of a work of art, and Merriam-Webster would try to describe it in a single word.

"Kinker," tweeted @merriamwebster in response to @

LACMA's sculpture of a leaping man. "A kinker is 'an acrobat or other performer in a circus.'"

@LACMA then responded with another challenge: a stone-and-metal mask from Alaska that vaguely resembles a bear with bright green gems as eyes. Picture a tribal leader dancing around the fire wearing this piece while praising a successful hunt or harvest.

"Ursine," responded @merriamwebster. "Ursine means 'of or relating to a bear or the bear family (Ursidae)' or 'suggesting or characteristic of a bear.'"

Continuing their process of constant improvement, Merriam-Webster then reinvented the game once they saw the excited reactions of their fans. They reversed the game and began to ask LACMA to share a work of art based on a word the dictionary would share first.

"Hey @LACMA, how would you illustrate 'impedimenta'?" they tweeted, referring to a word that means "things that impede."

"No contest," the museum responded, sharing a painting of a woman wearing a comically wide dress, as if a table were stuffed underneath it.

"You've never looked better," the dictionary quipped.

Only on social media would a dictionary and a museum provide such entertaining banter, and only thanks to asking the right questions about themselves did such exceptional work happen.

"I had a conversation with someone who asked how I'd define our voice," Lisa recalled. "They were trying to make it retroactive, as if I sat there and said, '*This* is how our voice should be,' and I ticked off a bunch of boxes and passed it around the staff." She never hired a consultant or obsessed over some new technology to improve their results. She never issued a lengthy memo to demand that they manufacture a tone of voice. "None of that would have worked." Instead, she asked better questions.

It's easy to assume that Merriam-Webster's company and products are commodities. A dictionary is a dictionary, and a definition is a definition, regardless of which brand you choose. Could you really blame them for doing average work? However, thanks to their aspirational anchor, they've made it clear to the world that they're not your average dictionary.

Like Lisa and her team, we can all hone our intuition and determine what works best for us by asking the right questions about ourselves and our teams:

- Trigger question: What is my aspirational anchor?

(Combine your intent for the future and some kind of hunger you have today, whether you're dissatisfied with your own work, your company, your industry, or something else.)

- Confirmation question: What is your unfair advantage? (You are the biggest variable in your work. You and your team are the things that no competitor can access. That's your unfair advantage. Have you identified what specifically that advantage might be? Have you applied it to your work?)

"Think about the advice you get as a child: Be you. No one else can be you," Lisa said.

Just by existing in your work, you inevitably change it. On the other hand, best practices encourage you to stop trying to be yourself. They provide the mold and the method, and we are mere servants of those lists and blueprints. A best practice is supposed to work regardless of who executes them. By their very nature, they eliminate your importance to the work. This is ignoring a powerful truth: *you* are the biggest variable in your work.

"The only reason it works is because it's not a marketing construct," Lisa said. "It's who we really are."

Now, in all of this talk about being yourself, I can sense some celebration fireworks going off in your gut. If you're the kind of person who loves the advice to "just be you," it's tempting to simply run with that advice. But *you* aren't the only element of your context that deserves investigation in order to make the right decisions.

"Here's a really important point that everybody misses," Scott told me. "If I was getting no gigs, if I was getting no paid keynotes, I would wear a tuxedo." On stage, Scott is true to himself not only because it feels good, but because it actually delivers results. He's making money. He's found the Venn diagram overlap between who he is and what his audience wants. Because it's not enough to understand yourself. You have to understand your audience too. That's the next part of our context to understand.

So what are the right questions we can ask about our audience? To find them, let's travel back in time to a tropical island facing a big problem. There, we'll meet the individual locals called "The Parrot Man of the Caribbean."

* * *

INVESTIGATE YOUR CONTEXT

Ask the right questions to hone your intuition
and make the best decisions for your situation
(regardless of the best practice).

PIECE OF YOUR CONTEXT	TRIGGER QUESTION	CONFIRMATION QUESTION
You	What is your aspirational anchor?	What is your unfair advantage?
Your Audience	(Chapter 5)	(Chapter 5)
Your Resources	(Chapter 6)	(Chapter 6)

CHAPTER 5

INVESTIGATE YOUR AUDIENCE

In the Eastern Caribbean sits a tiny island called St. Lucia. In the heart of the island sits an old wooden sign. And on the sign sits a simple message, written in black paint, cracked and faded: "Remember to take nothing but photographs, leave nothing but footprints, kill nothing but time."

Today, most people obey those words, but years ago, people took far more than photographs, and they didn't just kill time.

This sign welcomes visitors to the Barre de L'Isle Trail, a strenuous hike through the rainforest and up Mount La Combe, past two miles of leafy green plants, below the endless squawking of tropical birds. To most people (and birds), the welcome sign is insignificant. But to one man (and his favorite bird), this sign symbolizes years of hard work. That is, if you can call dancing and singing in a parrot costume hard work.

In 1977, Paul Butler was a long-haired, bespectacled student at Northeast London Polytechnic. As the Earth Island Journal would later describe him, young Paul was like "Mr. Rogers on speed." He was warm, earnest, and unstoppably exuberant—all traits he would need on a trip to St. Lucia during his final year of school. He arrived at the island to study the decline of a specific population of the St. Lucia parrot. Little did he know that this trip would be the first step in becoming a conservation legend. But to understand Paul's rise to industry fame, we first need to know two things: the bizarre trend surrounding the St. Lucia parrot, and a concept known as *homo economicus.*

The St. Lucia parrot has piercing red eyes surrounded by deep blue feathers that fade to teal around its head. The rest of the bird is mostly neon green, while shocks of red on its chest and under its wings match the parrot's eyes. The beautiful species is the living embodiment of "tropical rainforest." But the St. Lucia parrot is also a bastard. The bird emits a wide array of harsh noises, squawking and clicking and croaking and screeching at offensively loud volumes. When you hear these parrots, you don't think, "Hey, that's a bird." You think, "Hey, someone is murdering a bird." So it's no surprise that St. Lucian residents often treated these birds like pests, killing them with slingshots when they invaded their yards or the trees surrounding their businesses.

But the problem didn't stop there. Due to the struggling economy, poorer residents would often kill and eat the birds. To earn a living, others would capture them and try to sell them as pets—apparently to human beings without ears. *(Brawwwk!)* To locals, these parrots clearly weren't precious creatures—they were tropical pigeons. As a result, they were killed, eaten, and captured to the point of near extinction. In 1977, Paul Butler estimated just 150 were left alive in the wild.

To try to reverse this troublesome trend, Paul wrote a massive report to the government of St. Lucia. The document urged the Forestry Department to protect the parrot. He identified all kinds of ways they could do so: updating outdated legislation, creating and enforcing harsher penalties for hunters, and forming a sanctuary to protect the species. In his report, Paul followed arguably the most prevalent best practice in environmental conservation. While it convinced the Forestry Department to take action, the report alone wouldn't be enough to save the species. Like most best practices, this report was simply a decent place to start.

Paul had done the easy part. He'd convinced the government the bird needed saving. But he knew the real test would be changing people's behavior. The island's residents had created the problem. They'd need to be the ones to solve it. This simple realization helped Paul push past the average approach in his field and achieve something exceptional.

It's here that we need to know the second detail about Paul's story: a concept known as *homo economicus* or "the economic man." The concept stipulates that human beings are rational, self-interested, and labor-averse creatures. It was formally introduced by British philosopher John Stuart Mill in the late nineteenth century, although eighteenth century thinkers like Adam Smith and David Ricardo frequently wrote about the same principles. For instance, in *The Wealth of Nations*, Smith writes, "It is not from the benevolence of the butcher, the brewer, or the baker that we expect our dinner, but from their regard to their own interest." Why do these people sell us meat, ale, and bread? Is it because they're being nice to us? Of course not. It's because they're earning a living. They're self-interested.

For decades, *homo economicus* informed the approaches of environmental conservationism. If humans are rational and self-interested, then the logical way to change their behavior is to provide the right incentives and punishments. Thus, conservationists focused much of their efforts on local and federal lawmakers. They'd lobby the government to create rewards for protecting the environment and penalties for harming it.

But Paul Butler had spent time around the people of St. Lucia. He recognized that these weren't simply rational or self-interested creatures. They also believed in community and loved their families and friends. Most of all, they were proud of their home. Paul experienced a kind of local pride that he hadn't seen anywhere else in the world. One could argue that at this particular time in history, no people in the world were as proud of their home as St. Lucians. Understanding this detail would prove crucial to Paul's willingness to question *homo economicus.*

In February of 1979, just two years after Paul first arrived on the island, St. Lucia received its independence from the United Kingdom. Celebrations were planned and elections were held. A wave of national identity spread across the 150,000 residents of this newly minted country. Everywhere Paul looked, he saw St. Lucian culture and community on full display. He realized that these people weren't cold and calculating. They were emotional.

That is a great example of a first-principle insight. First-principle insights are fundamental but hard-to-reach truths about your context. Think back to your last physics class. (Okay, don't. That's too traumatic. I'll just remind you.) First principles are the foundational truths you need to grasp in order to build up any theory or idea. If we can cut through conventional wisdom and reason from first principles, we can inform our decisions using better insights about the world around us.

Tim Urban, creator of the popular site Wait But Why, has written multiple essays on first-principle thinking. His first was "The Cook and the Chef: Musk's Secret Sauce," a profile of Elon Musk, the founder and CEO of Tesla and SpaceX and previously a cofounder of PayPal. In the piece, Urban likens people who make decisions through conventional wisdom to cooks, while those who reason through first principles he calls chefs.

"Everything you eat—every part of every cuisine we know so well—was at some point in the past created for the first time. Wheat, tomatoes, salt, and milk go back a long time, but at some point, someone said, 'What if I take those ingredients and do this...and this...and this...' and they ended up with the world's first pizza. That's the work of a chef."

Chefs start with raw ingredients and then try to figure out what they can create with them. Cooks, however, may see the ingredients, but they rarely try to use them to concoct anything new. They see some wheat, tomatoes, salt, and milk, and they think pizza. They follow previously established recipes, going far enough to make those recipes their own, but not so far as to create anything truly original.

"Cooks span a wide range," Urban writes. "On one end, you have cooks who only cook by following a recipe to the T—carefully measuring every ingredient exactly the way the recipe dictates. The result is a delicious meal that tastes exactly the way the recipe has it designed. Down the range a bit, you have more of a confident cook—someone with experience who gets the general gist of the recipe and then uses her skills and instincts to do it her own way. The result is something a little more unique to her style that tastes like the recipe but not quite. At the far end of the cook range, you have an innovator who makes her own concoctions. A lamb burger with a vegetable bun, a peanut butter and jelly pizza, a cinnamon pumpkin seed cake."

In other words, the difference is the degree to which some copy and some create.

According to Urban, Elon Musk calls the cook's decision-making process "reasoning by analogy." On the other hand, when Musk makes decisions, he reasons through first principles. He tries to ask "Why?" and investigate his situation so thoroughly that he finds truths that are basic yet hard to reach. Then, he builds up his original thinking from there.

> **The difference is the degree to which some copy and some create.**

For instance, through his company SpaceX, Musk wants to colonize Mars. To colonize Mars, he has to make space travel relatively affordable for at least some wealthy people. When he first started, rockets were impossibly expensive—so expensive that his goal seemed unattainable. Then Musk asked "Why?" enough times to reach some very powerful first principles that his peers hadn't considered—or at least taken seriously enough to inform their decisions. He realized rockets are impossibly expensive because so many parts and pieces are sold to his competitors from different companies, all of which want to maximize their profits. As a result, when he launched SpaceX, Musk decided to bring the production in-house, becoming a "vertically integrated" operation. He also realized that the price of a ticket on a spaceship could drop even further if a rocket could be reused, much like an airplane. We can afford to fly on airplanes because our tickets don't need to cover the cost of the entire plane. Musk recognized that the key was the ability to land the vehicle, fix it and fuel it, then launch it again. So rather than focus SpaceX solely on rockets reaching orbit, Musk allocated resources to design and test vehicles that could successfully land on Earth without breaking apart.

"Conventional wisdom is slow to move, and there's significant lag time between when something becomes reality and when conventional wisdom is revised to reflect that reality," Urban writes. "And by the time it does, reality has moved on to something else. But chefs don't pay attention to that, reasoning instead using their eyes and ears and experience. By ignoring conventional wisdom in favor of simply looking at the present for what it really is and staying up-to-date with the facts of the world as they change in real-time—in spite of what conventional wisdom has to say—the chef can act on information the rest of us haven't been given permission to act on yet."

IT'S ONLY CRAZY IN SEATTLE

Even when you're not building something from scratch, you can still act like a chef. That's what we can learn from the more recent growth of Starbucks in China.

The company's founder and CEO, Howard Schultz, has talked publicly about their initial struggles to penetrate that market. "We lost money for nine consecutive years," Schultz said on *Masters of Scale*, a podcast hosted by Silicon Valley legend Reid Hoffman. "During that time, as a public company, [investors] said, 'This isn't working. You're losing money. It's a tea-drinking society. Close it up.'"

Until the struggles in China, the key to Starbucks' success, according to Schultz, was employee happiness. They hired driven, career-focused people. They offered good benefits. They treated each employee well so, in turn, they'd treat each customer well. But in China, they had experienced alarming employee attrition. As a result, business didn't take off. That's when Schultz and his team investigated the situation in more detail to identify a powerful first-principle insight: they had to appeal to employees' parents.

"Eighty-seven percent of our employees in China then and today are college graduates," Schultz said, "and the parents in China, especially given the one-child rule, are deeply involved in the lives and the aspirations of their children."

Schultz discovered that the typical parent wasn't convinced Starbucks was a great place to work. "They felt, 'I sent my son or daughter to college, and they're serving coffee as opposed to working for Apple or Google or Alibaba or Tencent. Why are they working at Starbucks? It's not right.'"

Schultz consulted his Chinese employees and a trusted friend, Jack Ma, the CEO of Alibaba and the richest man in China. They all confirmed the same thing. If Starbucks didn't serve the parents, they wouldn't hire or retain happy employees. Without happy employees, the company wouldn't deliver exceptional customer service. And without that level of service, the brand was doomed to struggle in China. So Starbucks did something that seemed rather unthinkable to a company in the United States: they offered benefits not just to their employees but to their employees' parents. Schultz even took this one step further. He decided to have an annual meeting of the parents of Starbucks employees in China.

"The people sitting in Seattle, when I said those words, I think they thought I was crazy," Schultz said.

Today, Starbucks is thriving throughout China. The number of stores exploded from 700 to 3,200, across 135 cities, over the last five years. A new Starbucks opens every fifteen minutes in the country, and the company boasts over 600 locations in Shanghai alone. It's the highest number of Starbucks in any city globally. Their first-principle insight about their Chinese employees proved to be a crucial factor in their growth. Initially, the leaders at Starbucks reasoned by analogy. *This worked in the United States. It will work like that in China too.* It took nearly a decade, but Starbucks began making better decisions by breaking from their own internal conventions—best practices that hadn't taken into account the variables of a new context.

"The challenge is, when you get this big, how do you

maintain the intimacy [you had] when you knew all the people and you were hungry and fighting?" Schultz said. "These kinds of moments are so emotionally alive with the spirit and culture and values of the company. And what we learned is that we are longing for human connection. We're longing for a sense of humanity and kindness and compassion and empathy."

In June of 2018, Starbucks announced that Howard Schultz was stepping aside as the company's chairman. In a statement released by the company, he said, "I set out to build a company that my father, a blue-collar worker and World War II veteran, never had a chance to work for. Together we've done that, and so much more, by balancing profitability and social conscience, compassion and rigor, and love and responsibility."

Whether we're veteran leaders affecting global economies or we're just taking our first steps in our careers, we can all inform our decisions using these basic but hard-to-reach truths about our audience. That is the trigger question to better understand others: **what is your first-principle insight?**

What is the core issue or fact that you've learned about those you aim to serve? Whether you're investigating your prospects or customers, your readers or viewers, or your employees or bosses, support your intuition by cutting through the conventional understanding about your audience. Howard Schultz realized that his Chinese employees' careers were heavily informed by their parents' wishes. Without addressing that fact, the company may have continued to languish in the Chinese market.

Similarly, on the island of St. Lucia, environmental conservationist Paul Butler realized that humans weren't rational creatures. Instead, he extracted the first-principle insight of his audience: humans are emotional. It seems so simple, but that's the beauty of these types of insights. They tend to be basic. They're foundational. But we operate in a world full of so much conventional wisdom and advice that we can lose sight of the basic elements of our work. Thus, we need to take the time to ask ourselves: what is our first-principle insight about the audience?

By answering that question, Paul Butler determined that the concept of *homo economicus* had created several best practices that simply weren't the right approach in his situation. For decades, conservationists relied on this notion of the logical, rational human to implement rewards and punishments. When people refused to comply with these new regulations, those people were deemed criminals. Conservationists would demonize them. But on the island of St. Lucia, Paul had witnessed something far more nuanced than "bad guys killing birds." He saw families struggling to survive.

Many people in St. Lucia were poor. To survive, they often hunted local birds for food. Other times, they'd clear large swaths of land to plant crops. This would cause both near-term damage to local fauna, eliminating much of their habitat, and long-term damage to the island as cleared land running up the mountains was more likely to flood. Because Paul spent so much time trying to understand the motivations and daily lives of others on the island, he no longer saw this behavior as incriminating.

Given the reality of his audience, Paul knew that the typical approach wouldn't work. He needed to do something stronger than just stand on his soapbox to demand change. In reasoning from first principles, Paul found a solution that not only affected St. Lucia but eventually helped more than fifty countries worldwide struggling with environmental issues.

So what did Paul do? He launched a Pride Campaign. It started with a mascot he created called Jacquot the parrot. Sometimes, Jacquot would appear as a human-sized mascot—the supersized version of the bird that needed saving. However, in every appearance, whether plush or printed, Jacquot represented something far bigger than a bird. He became a symbol of the nation's new sense of pride. Through marketing messages and community events across the island, Paul explained how this bird was a crucial part of the national identity. It wasn't merely a nuisance, a source of food, or a prospective pet. By associating the St. Lucia parrot with an emotion others felt, rather than a problem they had to solve, Paul believed he could genuinely change people's behavior.

"Too many conservation programs are run by scientists," he later explained to the journal *American Birds*. This made no sense to him. A car brand doesn't ask its engineers to sell cars, so why do conservationists turn to scientists to educate and persuade? If people make decisions based on emotions, sharing a bunch of facts and figures wouldn't work. He needed to act more like a marketer than a typical conservationist.

"Instead of using a sexy chick to sell cigarettes, we're using a sexy bird to sell conservation," Paul joked.

Thus, Jacquot was born. Paul would dress up to look like the bird, donning a colorful costume like he was about to roam the stands at a baseball game. The stakes may have been higher than the Yankees playing the Orioles, but Paul's role was no different: he was there to rouse the crowd. At community events and school assemblies, Paul encouraged thousands of St. Lucians to dance and sing songs about their wonderful island—and the wonderful bird that called the island home. He ran ads, posted flyers, handed out pamphlets, and created t-shirts reading "Pride of St. Lucia." He even helped improve the economy so that locals would stop eating the animal.

Using the momentum of the Pride Campaign, Paul worked with government officials to get the parrot selected as the official national bird. This meant that locals couldn't eat it, which could potentially harm many poorer individuals living in the jungle and along mountain trails. So Paul helped establish and promote hiking trails as tourist attractions to inject the region with more revenue.

"It's economic empowerment," he said. "These trails can generate a lot of income. It shows both the government and the locals they can make money from the forest and the birds without consuming them." After the Pride Campaign, the forest's abundant plant life prevented the loose earth from ruining the trails. Paul estimated that the main trail alone could generate $250,000 in fees from visitors each year. In the years that followed St. Lucia's independence, thousands of tourists paid tens of thousands of dollars to purchase refreshments and food from citizens of St. Lucia. Even the construction of the trail employed more than eighty locals for over two years.

In the years that followed the campaign, the parrot population grew by over 400 percent.

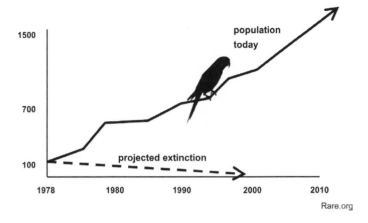

Rare.org

Today, about a third of the island is forested, and half of that land is now protected in government-preserved jungle. This jungle is home to a now-thriving population of St. Lucia parrots, which squawk and screech and click happily over the heads of people hiking through trails marked by worn wooden signs with cracked paint.

"Remember to take nothing but photographs, leave nothing but footprints, kill nothing but time."

Thanks to Paul Butler and his first-principle insight, that's exactly what people do.

It would be misleading to cite just one reason that Paul succeeded and St. Lucia experienced an economic resurgence. However, triggering a domino effect this massive required that Paul and his associates tip over that first domino. Without truly understanding the audience, Paul would never have created a Pride Campaign. Without identifying a first-principle insight, Paul would have started his thinking in a worse place, and he would have created an average campaign.

Now the question becomes: How do you know that your insight is correct? How do you know it's something worth pursuing?

IS YOUR FIRST-PRINCIPLE INSIGHT CORRECT?

As we attempt to make intuition a practical tool, we've identified two questions to ask about yourself and/ or your team, and one question to ask about your intended audience.

Questions about You:

- Trigger question: what is your aspirational anchor?
- Confirmation question: what is your unfair advantage?

Questions about Your Audience:

- Trigger question: what is your first-principle insight?

But here's another question: how can you tell when you've identified a first-principle insight? If we're strapped to this endlessly spinning wheel of best practices, how can we know for sure that we've broken free? Very simply, we need to pay more attention to the emotions of others. We're so obsessed with getting a big result that we undervalue a small number of people reacting to our work in a big way. That may not be what we consider final success, but it's a powerful signal that we're on the right path.

In the case of Paul Butler, the difference between the conventional approaches (projects inspired by *homo economicus*) and his Pride Campaign (inspired by his first-principle insight) was his focus on triggering a strong emotional reaction. Although the path was unconventional compared to what most conservationists did, Paul proceeded with confidence, not because he immediately saw results, but because he immediately saw an emotional reaction from a few people. Paul had found his true believers.

True believers are early and vocal supporters of your work, and they can provide the confirmation we need that our first-principle insight is accurate. After all, if you address the foundational problem or desire of an audience, you'll likely see a more powerful reaction. It's as if others are throwing up their hands and saying, "Finally! You get me! This is what I've been seeking all along!"

> **We're so obsessed with getting a big result that we undervalue a small number of people reacting to our work in a big way.**

I first learned about true believers from Lee Hower, a veteran technology entrepreneur and cofounding partner at NextView Ventures. I worked at the VC firm for three years as their vice president of content and community (what they call "platform" in VC). It was there that Hower first shared his perspective on the idea: "I'm fond of saying that raising capital for a startup (or any risky, early-stage venture for that matter) is not about convincing the skeptics, but rather finding the true believers."

There's a common misconception that entrepreneurs are great at convincing others to see the world their way. In reality, they're masters of rallying others who already believe what they believe.

"The entrepreneur's natural impulse is to try to persuade," Hower said. "This does occasionally happen. Lightning also does occasionally strike twice in the same spot, and people occasionally win the lottery. In general though, it's a massive waste of time trying to convince an already skeptical investor."

Lee Hower should know. NextView has invested in more than sixty internet startups, adding a dozen new investments to its portfolio each year. Additionally, Hower learned from some of the best minds in the history of tech entrepreneurship. In 2000, Elon Musk hired Hower to his company X.com, which later merged with Peter Thiel's startup Confinity to form PayPal. After eBay acquired PayPal for $1.5 billion, Hower joined the founding team of a new venture from former PayPal COO Reid Hoffman called LinkedIn.

Throughout his career, both as an entrepreneur and an investor, Hower has seen the power of rallying true believers. In 2011, he immortalized the idea with a short but powerful blog post titled "In Search of True Believers." In the piece, he writes, "Successful fundraising outcomes are produced by navigating to those true believers, rather than convincing skeptics. Remember that and allocate time accordingly." Hower is talking about a specific kind of true believer: investors.

Ever since I learned about this concept, however, I've noticed the power of finding true believers cropping up all over the business world. Whenever a company differentiates itself from the competition or sparks a movement in the market, I've stopped believing that some genius idea or massive budget led to their success. Whenever you look under the hood, you tend to see that the company began by finding a small number of people reacting in a big way to something they created. They let their true believers show them the path forward. That's exactly what Clair Byrd did.

UNCONVENTIONAL DOESN'T MEAN RISKY

For three years, Clair worked as a marketing manager at the software company InVision, which sells tools to help digital product designers create and share prototypes of websites and apps. As marketers, Clair and her team faced a common problem: InVision's niche is incredibly saturated with competitors. In addition to InVision, designers can use Sketch, Zeplin, Marvel, Axure, Figma, MockFlow, Balsamiq, Webflow, Flinto, Framer, RapidUI, Hype 3, Principle, NinjaMock, Pencil, and HotGloo... just to name a few. Clair's problems only got worse from there, as all of these companies look and sound extremely similar. Each company sells prototyping tools for designers. Each company claims to make collaboration and communication easier for teams. Each company professes to be the best and most widely beloved brand in the space.

"Join over 3 million designers," reads the InVision website.

"Industry Leader," brags Axure's home page.

"You'll be in good company," reads a Marvel page that lists a bunch of sexy client logos.

Suffice it to say, differentiation is an industry problem. Every competitor tends to look rather average. However, thanks to Clair Byrd approaching a pretty average tactic in an exceptional way, InVision has become the exception.

It all began with Clair identifying a first-principle insight. She was creating customer case studies for the company website—a common best practice—when she noticed something about her clients. Clair wanted to get her customers' perspectives on where product design was headed as a career path in tech companies. Almost immediately, they'd get defensive. They would argue passionately— angrily even—about why product design was undervalued in the business world, as if these design leaders had to justify their positions to their bosses. So, while InVision's customers answered positively when Clair asked about their tools, they would practically pound their chests in defense of their jobs once the conversation shifted to the broader software industry. Clair wondered, what was happening here? Something deeper was going through their minds. To figure that out, she ditched the conventional playbook and began to act more like an investigator.

Why are they getting defensive? Because they want to be taken more seriously at work.

Why don't others take them seriously now? Because they don't understand the value of product design.

Why don't they understand the value of product design? Because they don't know what product designers even do.

Around this time, in 2016, "product designer" wasn't a well-known title. That's when Clair found her first-principle insight: *product design needs an identity.*

If that was the case, InVision had a massive opportunity. They could rally the community together around their brand, not by creating more case studies or promotional content, but by making their brand the focal point for the industry's true believers. As a marketer, Clair's job wasn't to sell software. In reality, the job was to give product designers an identity. Once her team decided to do that, InVision sold a ton of software.

Thanks to the passionate responses they'd witnessed from InVision's customers, the marketing team pursued an unconventional path with more confidence. In the end, they didn't create another average case study. In fact, they didn't create a case study at all. Over the next few months, Clair and her team produced *Design Disruptors*, an hour-long documentary film about the craft and career of product design.

The film opens in stunning fashion, with a low-but-rising synth noise and some radio static as a hidden voice explains why design matters. The loud strum of an electric guitar breaks the low hum of the synth music, and several new voices start passionately explaining how design affects billions of people around the world.

"I think of design as a bridge that connects complexity with meaning," said Dropbox's head of design, Alex Castellarnau. "On one side, you have something complex. It could be a technology, could be a system, could be anything. On the other side, you have a person. Design is that thin layer that connects complexity to meaning."

Suddenly, we're flying over a bridge while a fuzzy white line shoots from one side to another, like God is drawing with chalk on the surface of the planet.

"If you can create an amazing experience, it's going to help improve your business," explained Andy Law, the director of mobile product design at Netflix. "I think that wasn't something that was so clear even five years ago."

Design Disruptors is beautiful and dramatic, casting designers as the heroes of the story. It features leaders from companies shaping the lives of billions of people today: Google, Facebook, Twitter, Salesforce, Dropbox, MailChimp, Airbnb, Lyft, Netflix, and more. They all appeared because InVision rallied together these true believers. They didn't want to help market InVision's brand. They wanted to help create an identity for their community.

"Maybe three years ago, designers were always worried about being at the table," said Jenny Arden, user experience designer at Google. "We were always complaining that we don't have a voice, people don't listen to us, engineers have the upper hand. It's not the case anymore. In fact, if you're a designer that believes you don't have a seat at the table, you're not listening."

To this day, *Design Disruptors* has never aired publicly. Instead, InVision held private screenings and meetups to attract more true believers. In more than 450 cities across the globe, InVision customers, prospects, and community groups supporting designers partnered with the company to show the film live. In total, they held more than 1,000 screenings. By bringing together passionate designers and leaders from top companies, InVision built real relationships with potential customers, generating more than 70,000 highly qualified sales leads in the process. Today, brands like Amazon, HBO, and IBM use InVision. NBC even invited InVision's team into their offices to conduct design workshops and talk about the film.

"The goal in making the film was to provide a foundational piece of content for the design community that described the importance of design and the impact that it has in the marketplace today," Clair said.

I asked Clair why she called the film a foundational piece for the "design community" instead of "for the company." Her response: "[InVision] is there to help people do their jobs better, not to try to enforce a specific type of design within an organization."

Design Disruptors contributed to InVision's fast rise as they more than doubled their users to over 2 million in a single year. As of the summer of 2018, the company had raised over $235 million in venture capital funding, the most in their industry. I wasn't there for the investor pitches, but something tells me they didn't try to convince any skeptical VCs. In everything InVision does, they seem to rally true believers.

It's worth acknowledging here that InVision employs a group of rather creative people. They've spent years building up the muscle memory of creating content and serving designers. I recognize that your situation might be different. Maybe you work in a more conservative industry or conventional company and thus suffer through more red tape and political jockeying than the InVision team. If that's you, your true believers might not be your customers, at least not at first. Instead, you should focus on internal stakeholders like bosses and influential executives. That's what Michael Brenner discovered the hard way.

THE BIG MISSING EMOTION

Today, Michael Brenner is marketing-industry-famous. He's a keynote speaker, author, and content marketing consultant. More than 100,000 people follow him on Twitter. Forbes named him a top CMO influencer. Huff-Post called him one of the world's best business speakers. But early in Michael's career, he struggled to convince others to do anything but cling to conventional thinking.

Like Clair Byrd at InVision, Michael was a marketing manager. Unlike Clair, he worked for the global tech giant SAP. They're no nimble, creative startup. They're a massive organization, employing more than 91,000 people who serve 388,000 customers in 180 countries. SAP generates $28 billion in annual revenue. At one point in his career, Michael Brenner felt the crippling weight of all of that pushing down on him.

It all started when the CEO of SAP, Bill McDermott, delivered a speech to 20,000 customers and prospects at a company event in Orlando. Rather than describe SAP's product updates, he focused on how technology trends affected businesses across the world. The talk was so well-received that McDermott immediately asked the company's marketing leadership why they didn't market that way, rather than talk exclusively about SAP's products. The CMO turned to Michael Brenner and asked if he'd solve that problem. Thus, a CEO asked a CMO, who then asked a manager to do something. You can't get more top-down approval for something than that.

"This is going to be easy and fun," Michael recalled thinking at the time. "It turned into anything but."

Michael dove into the company's data and found a horrible problem: almost nobody in the world visited the SAP website without first knowing SAP's brand. Traffic estimation tools from Google revealed that 30,000 percent more people searched for topical keywords rather than SAP's brand terms. That's not a typo. Thirty. Thousand. Percent. These keywords described SAP's product *categories*, like "cloud computing" and "big data," rather than the brand itself. Naturally, Michael presented these findings to his superiors, along with his suggestion that SAP should begin to publish educational blog content about those terms in order to rank on Google search results. But then a strange thing happened.

"I actually got pretty personal and enthusiastic pushback," he said. "It was pretty violent."

All of his colleagues believed that SAP should only be

marketing to individuals who already knew their brand and were one step away from buying their products. That had been their playbook for decades. Why should they change now?

Three separate times, Michael parsed the data and presented his findings and suggestions to SAP's marketing leaders. Three separate times, they turned him away. In fact, by the third time, Michael says that instead of passionate pushback, he was met with total apathy. People simply tuned him out and went about their days, running the old, conventional marketing playbook.

After weeks of agonizing over the problem, Michael realized it was his fault, not theirs. He had been trying to convince the skeptics rather than rallying true believers. The fourth time he presented to his peers and bosses would be his last, because at long last, people listened. So what changed? He told a better story.

"We need to figure out why we're doing what we're doing," Michael told me. "Data can't answer that for anyone. Getting to the narrative is about asking a series of whys until there's nowhere else to go."

Data is obviously useful, but blind reliance on *numbers* often poses a problem. Sure, you can win hands playing poker by the numbers, but to be the best, you have to play the other people at the table too. That may sound a bit nefarious, but I mean it with the best of intentions: we need to focus on the people on the other end, not merely the cold, hard facts. To rally others behind your cause or your idea, you need to have a compelling narrative.

Narratives contain three simple components: a status quo, some conflict, and a resolution. This applies whether you're a child singing with friends in preschool or an executive making billion-dollar decisions. The itsy-bitsy spider went up the water spout, but then that damn rain washed him out. Then the sun came out, and he went back up there successfully. Good on him! That's your status quo-conflict-resolution. For SAP, the status quo was focusing on customers almost ready to buy, who knew the brand already. But in the digital age, the buyer had changed. Customers had all the power because they had access to all the information. They were searching on Google, reading blogs, downloading reports, watching explainer videos, and browsing case studies. They'd changed, but SAP had not adjusted accordingly. That's some serious conflict. Michael used that conflict to construct a better, more convincing narrative to his colleagues. More specifically, he told a story using one powerful emotion: fear.

"Our competitors are beating us," he told his bosses. "The customer has changed the way they buy thanks to technology, but we have not evolved how we go to market.

We're in danger of falling behind the competition, who are already blogging and creating helpful content. They are capturing that traffic on Google, and we are not."

At long last, he received the executive endorsement he needed to work with marketing teams throughout the organization and implement a global content marketing strategy. Soon after, Michael was promoted from a regional marketing manager to a vice president. He became a globally recognized leader in marketing, appearing on webinars, in articles, and on stages all across the industry as thousands of brands tried to understand this new "content marketing" stuff. Today, after spending time as a consultant to many of those brands, Michael is the CMO of the tech company Concured and a globally touring keynote speaker.

"Data was half my life. It was always, 'Do X and see Y result.' And so I look back at this experience as one of the most intense and really most rewarding experiences because it reminded me of the power of story."

FINDING THE RIGHT TRAIL

It seems that those who do great things in their careers focus an inordinate amount of time on identifying true believers. Doing so leads to a snowball effect in your work, like an entrepreneur who uses their first yes from a single investor to gradually bring together more VCs into the fundraising round. In our journey to break from best practices and think for ourselves, what if we could generate a stronger, more emotional response from others? That could be the confirmation we need that our first-principle insight about our audience is correct. Thus, that's our confirmation question to continue honing our intuition about our audience: **Who are your true believers?**

Back on the island of St. Lucia, Paul Butler let his true believers guide his work. He took Jacquot the parrot on the road, attending more local events. He created more flyers and shirts using imagery of Jacquot. He partnered with the local government to get the mascot in front of more people. By continually reasoning from first principles, Paul did increasingly unconventional things to save the St. Lucia parrot.

Admittedly, I didn't see the Pride Campaign as all that crazy. Since I haven't spent years following the best practices of environmental conservation, when I first learned of Jacquot the parrot, I thought it was a refreshing and creative approach...but also a logical one. It was only unconventional to those who knew the convention. But here's an approach that will seem a bit crazy regardless of whether you're an industry insider: Paul believed that better family planning on St. Lucia could help save parrots, so he helped create a radio soap opera.

That's a lot to digest at once, so let's break it up to really bask in the weirdness. Paul believed that (A) teaching family planning through (B) a radio soap opera could (C) save more parrots?! And that's logical...how?

"It's a more holistic approach to environmental problems" he said. "The more condoms used, the more jungle and parrots we can keep."

Imagine Paul walking into a meeting of scientists and conservationists. "We must save the species!" he'd say. They'd all nod vigorously. "So I'm going to hand out condoms!" The nodding would stop right there.

When you reason from first principles, you tend to look a little crazy, because others lack the context you possess. Paul's context was simple but troubling: St. Lucia was struggling with overpopulation. No amount of dancing and singing with Jacquot the parrot could change that fact. Even if every citizen of the new nation of St. Lucia agreed to stop killing parrots, the growing number of people would eventually crowd out the birds, consuming the island's natural resources and clearing away their habitats. The Pride Campaign could help the species in the short term, but to truly save these parrots, Paul needed longer-term thinking.

Partnering with local radio stations, Paul helped bring a

radio soap opera to the island. It was a drama, but it acted as a sort of Trojan horse for Paul's message, exposing teenagers to the problems of early pregnancy and the benefits of smarter family planning. Although the numbers associated with the soap opera were not released publicly, the total sum of Paul's efforts seems to have worked. As I mentioned earlier, the St. Lucia parrot population grew by 400 percent in the short-term thanks to Paul's Pride Campaign. More critically, however, that number has remained steady in the decades since Paul arrived on the island.

In the late 1980s, Paul joined the environmental conservation organization Rare. To date, they've launched over three hundred Pride Campaigns globally, but here's the thing: the very nature of the Pride Campaign prevents Rare from simply repeating a tired best practice. In each location, the organization is forced to identify what, exactly, creates a sense of pride for locals. Rare can't merely copy and paste the tactic everywhere. Instead, the Pride Campaign prompts Rare's conservationists and global volunteers to continually investigate the specific context of each situation. Paul provided Rare with guardrails (a general direction) and goal posts (the desired outcome—i.e., behavior change). It doesn't prescribe each and every play to run. Sometimes, this even helps them decide when not to use a Pride Campaign at all.

"This campaign wouldn't work in the U.S.," Paul said. "There's just too much else going on." In other words, the volume of marketing messages Americans experience would prevent the Pride Campaign from standing out. "And if you dressed up like a spotted owl in the American northwest, someone would try to shoot you."

In the end, everyone we've learned about in this chapter did something that seems risky, creative, and maybe even a little insane. Their paths were unconventional. However, by asking the right questions about their audience, they made the unconventional path seem logical and even safe.

Intuition is not merely gut feel. It's the practice of thinking for yourself. However, while it's necessary to think better about your work, it's not sufficient. You also have to *act* in a way that produces your best work. If being exceptional requires finding and following what makes your situation an exception, then thus far, we've only done the "finding" part. Next, we need to understand how to follow what we've found. However, I should warn you: when we want to do great work so badly, this part may be our toughest challenge yet.

* * *

INVESTIGATE YOUR CONTEXT

Ask the right questions to hone your intuition and make the best decisions for your situation (regardless of the best practice).

PIECE OF YOUR CONTEXT	TRIGGER QUESTION	CONFIRMATION QUESTION
You	**What is your aspirational anchor?**	**What is your unfair advantage?**
Your Audience	**What is your first-principle insight?**	**Who are your true believers?**
Your Resources	*(Chapter 6)*	*(Chapter 6)*

CHAPTER 6

_____

INVESTIGATE YOUR RESOURCES

Mikael Cho is the CEO of a company called Crew.

Or at least, he was.

The Montreal-based entrepreneur is an upbeat guy who smiles with his eyes. His boyish look and optimistic nature make him rather magnetic. Unfortunately, in 2014, Mikael's company was heading in the polar opposite direction of what he wanted. He'd cofounded Crew as an online marketplace to connect website designers and developers to clients, but the business was burning more money than it could generate. They were running ads, building a following on social media, and publishing Google-friendly content to generate demand.

After the marketplace went live, however, few designers and developers signed up to feature their work, and even fewer companies visited the site to find a match for their projects. Nothing seemed to be working. As a result, the company had just three months' worth of cash left in the bank from an initial round of funding. The team was struggling to acquire customers, and VCs had shown zero interest in a new round of investment.

"We figured we weren't going to get a dime from anybody ever again," he said. "If we didn't turn things around, we were toast. Done."

The company was his baby, a source of incredible pride. Naturally, Mikael thought the same thing many of us might think when the usual tactics aren't working: "I have to do something new and creative." Now, what most of us picture when we hear those words—"new" and "creative"—is the wide open field. Total. Creative. Freedom! *You're telling me I get to be creative? I'm gonna go big! I'm gonna invent something the world has never seen! I'm gonna be the hero! I'm gonna write our message across the sky!*

But that's not what Mikael did. Instead, he put himself inside a box. He knew he had a list of constraints, each of which would have to inform his work.

He needed to build an audience for his business. (*Cool.*)

Targeting makers and marketers. (*Neat.*)

With no marketers on staff. (*Wait...*)

And no budget. (*Hold on...*)

In the next three months. Or else. (*I mean, what can you even do here?*)

Well, what Mikael did was rather restrained. He had to be responsible. He couldn't sprint wildly around the metaphorical field.

"I remember talking to my cofounder [Luke Chesser] over Skype, and I said, 'Hey, I have all these photos just sitting on my desktop from building Crew's website. Instead of them just sitting there, why don't we give them away?'"

Crew's target customers were in the process of building their own websites and apps. They could probably use some good photos. What if he offered them for free? Maybe he could attract potential customers to the company.

"Nobody at Crew thought this could work," Mikael said. "So I gave myself just one afternoon to work on it alone."

To house those photos online, Mikael opened a Tumblr

account, purchasing a template that allowed him to neatly arrange his photos into a grid. The design cost him nineteen bucks. Even a startup about to go out of business can afford that. Within four hours, Mikael had built the site, uploaded the photos, and given it a name: Unsplash.

"Free (do whatever you want) high-resolution photos," Mikael wrote on the top of the page. "Ten new photos every ten days."

Mikael's goal was to add as much value as he could to his customers' lives. Adding value is the core tenet of content marketing. In the past, marketing teams focused almost exclusively on messages about product features and benefits. Talking about yourself may have worked when the consumer had limited choice. Even if you didn't like a TV ad for soap, you only had a handful of additional channels and no secondary screen. Today, with a few clicks or quick glance to another device, we can minimize or circumnavigate unwanted ads, or even pay a small fee for ad-blocking software to remove them entirely.

According to a 2018 report by Deloitte, three out of four North American internet users practice some kind of ad-blocking behavior. By the end of the year, 10 percent of internet users over eighteen will engage in four or more ad-blocking behaviors, prompting the firm to coin the phrase "adlergic." Miserable portmanteaus aside, consumers simply don't tolerate miserable experiences any longer. Users have too much control. We also have too many options that allow for a better experience. Netflix, Hulu, and Amazon Prime Video offer programming void of ads while the premium subscription versions of You-Tube, Pandora, and Spotify let users eliminate unwanted messages for the same price as a cocktail at a trendy Manhattan bar.

For a business to reach customers today, they must become the object of people's choosing. People choose to spend time with things they believe will add value to their lives. Mikael Cho never forgot that.

On that fateful afternoon in 2014, Mikael knew he had to add value to attract an audience of makers and marketers who might use Crew to build websites or apps. If writing some articles about those subjects could add some value to the world, then offering a handful of beautiful stock photos for free would be even more enticing.

"We were looking for a way to add extreme value to help people find Crew," Mikael said. "I wanted to take things a step further."

Rather than execute any of the more typical tactics at the time, like blog posts, e-books, infographics, and other "pieces" of content, Mikael decided to create an interactive resource. He planned to give away those ten photos sitting unused on his desktop. Best of all, Mikael asked for nothing in return.

Unlike most brand websites, visitors experienced no forced forms or obnoxious calls-to-action on Unsplash. There was just a single spot to enter an email address if someone wished to subscribe. No matter how long you stayed on Unsplash or how many photos you downloaded, the company never bludgeoned you with a pop-up, demanding you fork over personal information to continue browsing. The lone company branding sat just below the website headline. There, in faded gray font, was a single hyperlink reading, "By Crew."

"There's a balance between adding value and asking for it." Mikael said. For instance, they could have watermarked each photo with the Crew logo, but according to him, "That would have ruined the entire project and the value we wanted to provide."

By focusing all his efforts on adding as much value as he could to his audience, Mikael created both a great experience that people loved and shared, *and* a powerful new marketing channel for Crew. The day he launched the site, he shared the link on Hacker News, an online forum of entrepreneurs run by the tech startup incubator Y Combinator. The forum receives more than 2 million visitors per day, and it operates much like Reddit: Users share links or ideas, which people can upvote. The more votes, the better the ranking on the forum. Readers can also add their own thoughts in threaded comments.

"That was my litmus test. I'd never really had success on Hacker News," Mikael told me.

After sharing the link on the discussion board, Mikael just continued working on other things for the rest of his day. He assumed there'd be no reaction from Hacker News. He also couldn't stand to look at the project once he launched it.

"I was so embarrassed about that first version," he said.

As afternoon turned to evening, Mikael heard from the photographer whose photos he'd uploaded to Unsplash earlier that day. "I got a text message and he said, 'Hey, where did you put those photos? My portfolio site is blowing up!'"

Mikael only put it in one place. He went back to Hacker News and discovered just about the last thing he expected to see: his post was the most upvoted link of the day. There it was, sitting at the top of the site's homepage.

That exposure drove 50,000 visitors to Unsplash in about

ten minutes. In the next twenty-four hours, Crew converted three times the customers they had in any single day prior. Over the next month, more than 20,000 Unsplash visitors subscribed via email to receive alerts when each new batch of photos went live. That email list proved crucial to Crew's survival as the company converted several paying customers.

After seeing an uptick in both prospective Crew users and paying Crew customers, Mikael went back out to fundraise from venture capitalists. Following months of futility prior to Unsplash, he was able to secure $2.1 million from a few investors, thus saving the company. And if you can believe it, this is where things got crazy.

The tech press picked up the story, and Mikael appeared in publications like The Verge, Fast Company, and Forbes. Next, Forbes began to use and credit Unsplash photography all across their website. This sent tens of thousands more people to the Unsplash site every week. Just two years later, in 2016, users downloaded photos more than 144 million times in a twelve-month span. By 2017, three photos were downloaded every second.

Within twenty-four months of launching Unsplash, the site had become a massive community, and it was Crew's top source of customer referrals. What had been just a few hours of Mikael's time uploading ten photos every ten days became a part-time role for his cofounder Luke Chesser. They added some basic functionality, like search and sorting. The more Unsplash improved, the more revenue Crew generated. In total, 20,000 projects were submitted to the Crew marketplace, or roughly $30 million in transactions, which helped double the company's revenue each year. Not too shabby for a company that had once struggled to get even a single project submitted.

Unsplash even spawned other side projects from Crew, like a cost estimation calculator for people considering building mobile apps and a master list of coffee shops conducive to remote work, sorted by city. A simple project turned into a company-saving revenue-generator, which turned into a teamwide culture of creating side projects to launch, learn, and grow. In the decade I've spent building things and serving creators, Unsplash is the most remarkable side project I've encountered.

It's easy to believe that something like Unsplash was all about creative freedom. But it wasn't. Indeed, we all want to sprint freely around that wide open field. But we shouldn't. It turns out that if you put enough boxes down on that field, you can cover just as much ground—and you can do so more successfully.

As Mikael realized, "When you need to be creative, constraints are your strengths."

THE PROBLEM WITH "CREATIVE FREEDOM"

When you understand your limitations (time, team, budget, skill, etc.), constraints force you to be realistic about what you can build. This, in turn, keeps you focused on building the *right* stuff.

But constraints aren't just helpful when it comes to building new things. They can also help you address existing processes in new and better ways. In 2015, a joint study from the University of Illinois and Johns Hopkins University concluded that a heightened sense of resource constraints led people to find more creative uses for products already at their disposal, compared to those who felt they had abundant resources.

Even more revealing, perhaps, is a 2009 study from the University of Iowa that examined the effects of physical boundaries on children. Researchers asked a group of kids to search for some carrots in a small field that they had hidden just out of site. One group was presented with a field that had no boundaries while three other groups were each given three different types of boundaries. The study revealed that the groups with boundaries executed a more organized and successful search for the carrots than those presented with zero boundaries. Said another way: when you want to do your best, constraints can help. It seems that creative freedom doesn't always work.

I'd argue creative freedom doesn't really exist. If I told you to write a blog post about anything you want, what's the first thing you'd do? You'd think about the topics and stories you want to address. You'd think about the length and the time of day you'll write, and where you'd physically sit (or stand). Maybe you'd think about how many hours it would take to write before submitting the piece. Or you'd decide whether to write an outline first or go straight to a Word doc. It's like your subconscious is telling you: *if we want to succeed here, we need to manufacture some constraints.*

In other words, when we embrace our constraints, we begin to scale our work based on results, not theory or trends. Who cares about the big idea in theory if it doesn't work for our audience? Who cares about the latest trend if it's not the best approach for our specific situation?

Mikael Cho fully embraced his constraints, not because he *wasn't* creative, but because he *was.* He looked for the box instead of the field, not because he *didn't* want to succeed, but precisely because he *did.* He wanted to be creative and succeed more desperately than anyone around him.

In 2017, Mikael announced the creation of Unsplash, Inc. The side project had grown so large that the team decided to spin it out into its own standalone company.

"I never expected this to happen," Mikael wrote on the company's new blog. "But then again...startups."

They split the team and their capital between two companies: Crew and Unsplash. But within just a few months, even that was no longer tenable. Unsplash continued to show so much promise that the cofounders decided to sell Crew. They found a good home in Dribbble (not a typo), the design portfolio community. What started as a four-hour afternoon, a nineteen-dollar Tumblr theme, and a bunch of old photos just sitting around, turned into the entirety of the team's focus. In early 2018, the newly formed company raised an additional $7.25 million to continue growing.

Mikael's journey illuminates the power of embracing our constraints rather than fighting them. If we try to create small tests and win each little battle, one at a time, we will continually learn, grow, and thrive—not because we buy into that myth of creative freedom, but because we embrace a more constrained approach to creativity. That's the reality of our work, after all. We'll never have total freedom, and that's okay.

Ask yourself this trigger question to investigate your resources: **what are your constraints?**

> **"When you need to be creative, constraints are your strengths."**
>
> **–Unsplash CEO Mikael Cho**

We don't like to accept that they exist. We prefer to complain, meet, advocate, and ask for more resources until we feel we have what we need to act. What if we truly understood our constraints instead? What resources do we already have? What are our goals? Our timeline? Team? Skills? Do we really understand our resources? If we did, we might have more success testing both our aspirational anchors and our first-principle insights. We'd make learning the goal rather than results, and in doing so, we might see better results.

For Mikael, when operating within his constraints, the stakes were high in one sense but low in another. They were high in that his company risked closing shop. This would affect his investors, a team of about thirty people, and of course, his pride. On the other hand, the stakes were low in that, if Unsplash failed miserably, very few people would notice.

When the stakes seem high or we're under more scrutiny from others, it's tempting to think that we need more resources before we can execute. *I need to create something with more polish than a minimally viable project. I could never have launched a small test and placed it on one website like Mikael.* And to that I'd say: you're correct, but only partially correct. The key is knowing *what parts of your work* should be constrained.

To understand what I mean, we first need to venture deeper into venture.

EMBRACING CONSTRAINTS WHEN THE STAKES ARE HIGH

"Venture" is shorthand for "venture capital." It's a common phrase insiders use to refer to their profession, which is something I learned while working in that industry for three years in Boston and New York, running the NextView Ventures brand. But something else I learned in venture ultimately showed me the power of embracing our constraints, even when the stakes are high. I learned about the work of Camille Ricketts at First Round Capital.

For context, First Round is one of the most prestigious early-stage VCs in the world. The firm was among the first investors in companies like Uber, Square, Blue Apron, OnDeck, and Warby Parker. In 2013, when they hired Camille Ricketts, their brand was already pristine and popular, but they feared losing the attention of their target audience: busy entrepreneurs. They knew they couldn't get complacent, and they believed content marketing was their best way to scale the value they could provide to startup founders.

Since First Round was already so well-known, Camille's first task—launching a company blog—came with a certain set of expectations, not to mention a ton of pressure. Unlike Mikael Cho with Unsplash, Camille couldn't just purchase a Tumblr template and call it a blog. Whereas Mikael could test in private and work his way to a polished, beautiful project, First Round is constantly scrutinized by investors, entrepreneurs, and tech journalists across the globe. Camille couldn't deliver anything less than a premium publication from the moment she launched.

Making matters harder for First Round, the competition was already fierce. Venture capitalists are notoriously prolific bloggers. They're deep thinkers, often with decades of experience in building startups, and the early VC bloggers like Fred Wilson, Mark Suster, and Brad Feld had become such household names that they created a trend. Hundreds of other investors began to blog in similar fashion, sharing perspectives on tech and entrepreneurship. There are so many VC blogs that the market intelligence firm CB Insights created the "Periodic Table of Venture Capital Blogs" just to help readers sort through the noise. The graphic lists eighty-nine different blogs that First Round would have to compete against, not to mention all the VCs who didn't make the list.

At first glance, launching a new blog as a venture capital firm seemed less than strategic. Why not attack an opportunity with fewer competitors? But once Camille began to investigate her audience more than her competition, it became clear that there was a gaping hole in the market that First Round could fill.

Before she identified that hole, Camille questioned whether the volume of VC blogs meant that entrepreneurs received sufficient value from them. The more she talked to founders, the more she realized that the early bloggers like Wilson, Suster, and Feld had given way to dozens of copycats, most incapable of replicating the value of those original three. It seemed that most VCs shared personal opinions and ideas pulled from their own experiences in the tech industry. Offline, however, Camille noticed that the most helpful investors didn't merely pull from their own experiences. After all, many had built businesses several years or decades prior, not in the current market. When Camille watched the interactions between First Round's partners and entrepreneurs, she realized that the most powerful exchanges didn't mimic those blogs posts. Instead, First Round added the most possible value when introducing founders they knew to others who could help them overcome tough challenges at their startups.

"What we thought would be a [blogging] niche in the

market that we hadn't seen filled yet was operators speaking to other operators," Camille said.

First Round's blog might succeed if they occupied that niche. Their articles would be an extension of the same value First Round's investors provided to founders every time they made an introduction offline: operators helping other operators. That would be the focus of their new blog, the First Round Review. That name captured the aspiration Camille carried with her since joining the firm: to create the Harvard Business Review for startups.

From the moment she was hired, Camille had been dreaming of building a new publication from the ground up. It would be something more elevated and premium than what most people imagine when they hear the word "blog." It would be a legitimate *magazine*. Over time, as she observed the behavior of her peers and her audience, she realized that this aspiration wasn't just empty fantasy. Creating the HBR of startups would fill a hole that still existed in the market.

"It occurred to us that there wasn't a resource for this type of information that was targeted so explicitly at startups," Camille said. "We saw an opening, and it was an easy way for us to describe what it was that we were doing."

Unfortunately, and despite the need to deliver a premium publication to the public from day one, Camille had almost no budget. She had zero writers on staff and was offered no help from the firm's partners on the project. She also figured she had roughly thirty days to prove the value of her approach to her bosses if she wanted to win more resources and continue building. Camille's situation was far from a wide-open field. It was a box, and a tiny one at that. However, once she embraced that reality, she started to thrive.

The first step was to create great content that required very little time, budget, or team. To do so, she began attending local startup events in her hometown of San Francisco. There, she'd seek out the most popular speeches from founders or executives—powerful examples of operators helping other operators.

"The earliest First Round Review stories were actually just recountings of speeches made at tech events," Camille said.

Just like Camille, if you start your decision-making process by understanding your context, you can build yourself a rather useful box to test your thinking. The first part of your context (you) and the second (your audience) can help you navigate the third (your resources). Given your existing context and resources, what can you do to succeed within the box? What is your version of Camille's speech transcriptions?

"That was our proving ground," she said. "Of course, it evolved from there."

Camille witnessed a small but passionate response to those early articles, including some founders who emailed her to praise the blog. "The best responses are when an entrepreneur tells us they forward our articles to their entire teams. That's the best result we can get."

To grow her budding publication, Camille held up these early wins as proof that the firm should give her more resources. She then used the extra budget to hire a writer. Together, they stopped transcribing speeches and started publishing original interviews with founders and executives from companies like Google, Spotify, Amazon, and Uber. When those interviews gained traction in both pageviews and passionate replies, she once again held up those results as a case study to her bosses to secure more resources. She then used those resources to build online community groups—forums for founders to ask and answer questions. It was a place for operators to help operators at scale. That proved to be a case study to secure even more resources. Today, First Round creates research reports, regular interviews, and even builds its own apps to help founders learn and grow.

Bit by bit, little by little, Camille Ricketts built something huge with First Round Review. Every month, over half a million readers visit the site. Their email list has ballooned to more than 150,000 subscribers, while tech media like Forbes, Pando, TechCrunch, and VentureBeat wrote excitedly about this "Harvard Business Review for startups."

At first, Camille faced a ton of competition in the VC blogosphere. Endless amounts of noise threatened to drown out First Round Review. But when your goal is to stand out, noise isn't the problem. Sameness is.

However, the goal isn't merely to create something "different." Anybody can be weird for no apparent reason. They key is doing something different and purposeful at the very same time. As a result, I believe aiming for "different" is missing the point. First Round Review isn't just different. It's refreshing, and I think refreshing is a far better goal for our work.

Just think: If our goal is to be different, our next question becomes, "Different from whom?" The competition. However, if our goal is to be refreshing, the next question is, "Refreshing *to* whom?" The customer! The audience. The people we aim to serve. They're the arbiter, the focus of our efforts. They're the reason we do our work, not the competition. As we've seen time and time again, when we pay more attention to the customer than to the competition, the customer pays more attention to us.

"Early on, some things will work, and some things won't, but you have to pay attention to what your audience is telling you they want," Camille said. "Your goal is to identify these 'value payloads,' or outlier successes that you can use to learn from and use to inform the rest of your work."

Once your audience reaction suggests that something is a value payload, you can invest with more confidence in that idea or approach. By testing, learning, and iterating quickly, you can scale your work based on actual results, not trends. After all, who cares what the competition is doing if it doesn't work for you? If we make learning the goal instead of end results, we might actually get our best results.

> **When we pay more attention to the customer than to the competition, the customer pays more attention to us.**

Once we've asked the trigger question about our constraints, we can then ask the confirmation question: **how might we expand?** We've identified our limitations and tested our way forward. Are we plucking what we've learned out of that first box and applying it to each and every new test we run? The goal isn't to expand from a box to a wide-open field but from one box to another in a lifelong process of learning and improving. That's what great investigators do. They move from one clue to another, updating their knowledge as much as possible.

"We're doing something that's incredibly helpful for other folks," Camille said. "It's not something you'd usually think you'd have the opportunity to do in the field of finance, which is to do something really altruistic."

In March of 2018, Camille decided to leave First Round Capital. After nearly five years building the Review, her ongoing process of testing, learning, and expanding will take her elsewhere, to an unannounced destination. She plans to take some time off to travel and see the world. When last we spoke, she'd just returned from a month in Bali and two weeks roaming around Central America. She seemed happy and rather self-assured that her decision to leave First Round was the right one.

It's as if Camille asked herself, "How might I expand upon what I've learned?" Once her investigation led her to a new job entirely, she left the best employer of her career with total confidence. Venture capital is a tough industry to join. It may seem crazy that Camille would leave, but that's the power of honing your intuition. When faced with a tough dilemma, you can make the right decision, regardless of what the conventional wisdom might dictate.

It seems that asking the right questions about your context can help with far more than launching your latest project. It can even change the trajectory of your entire career.

THE KEY TO EMBRACING CONSTRAINTS AT WORK

In our careers, we usually don't like to look our constraints in the eye. We prefer to advocate for more resources before we get started. Sometimes that devolves into stress or panic; other times, we resent gatekeepers like bosses or clients who hold the keys just out of reach. At our worst, however, we kick and scream about our lack of creative freedom. But that only reveals our lack of understanding of how great work happens. We don't need freedom. We need constraints. We need the box. Even more crucially, however, we need to articulate and agree on the *walls* of that box.

To team leaders:	To individual contributors:
Once you articulate and agree on the walls of the box, stay out of the box. Let your team innovate and create and test within those constraints. The entire reason you articulated them was to give people the freedom to investigate within those walls. The danger of the open field has been removed. Now it's on you as a leader to trust your team to execute, given those guardrails and goalposts. Usually, it's not the restrictions of the box that frustrate teams. It's the fact that their boss doesn't communicate those restrictions clearly enough, or she's too eager to jump inside of the box with them, or she keeps changing the list of constraints. If you're a leader, ensure your team understands what their limitations and goals are, and most importantly, why they exist. Get buy-in or clarity. Then get out of the way.	You also have a crucial role to play in investigating your resources. Arguably, it's your role to constantly and loudly ask the trigger question to people who decide your budget, timeline, and goals. Ask your boss or clients what the constraints are. Ask about money and time. Ask why the industry example inspired them to send it to you. Ask a ton of questions until the box has been made clear. There's nothing that will derail your work faster than running into an invisible wall. Ensure that doesn't happen. Bestselling author Seth Godin once described design thinking as asking three questions: Who is it for? What is it for? How will we know if it's working? If you're an individual contributor, use those questions and more to design the box.

Regardless of whether we're team leaders or individual contributors, our usual behavior is to replicate an action when we feel we've found "the" answer, because we now know what it takes. We know what the box looks like, so we can then forecast the resources we'll need more accurately.

We wrote a five-hundred-word blog post. It worked. Write more five-hundred-word blog posts.

We shipped a new feature in one week. It worked. Give all features a timeline of one week.

Instead, we need to keep running constrained tests. If something works, don't do more *like* it. Do more *with* it.

We wrote a five-hundred-word blog post. It worked. Great! Promote it to more places. Rip out the ideas from the copy and turn it into audio, video, or imagery. Use it to inspire deeper or tangential forms of education. Blow it out into an e-book. Make it your keynote speech or book. Don't do more like it. Do more with it to expand upon initial success.

We shipped a new feature in one week. It worked. Great! The reason the deadline led to great work wasn't the timing so much as the behavior it created. The team banded together as a unit. They worked in harmony, cheering each other on to meet that deadline. So let's also work that into team meetings, applauding good work more often. Let's highlight problems and conduct hackathons to fix them together. Don't make all deadlines one week. Don't do more like it. Do more with it.

Become a lifelong learner, a constant investigator. Hone your intuition by constantly testing everything. We may yearn for that wide-open field, but it turns out the more boxes we put down, the more ground we can cover. Eventually, we may look back and realize that little by little, we built something big.

Ask yourself the following questions to investigate the third and final part of your context, your resources:

- Trigger question: What are your constraints? (Do you fully understand what they are? Have you built yourself that box? The first two walls can be your aspirational anchor and your first-principle insight, which might come from firsthand learning. However, we need to work with our teammates, bosses, clients, and stakeholders to understand the guardrails and goalposts of a given job.)

- Confirmation question: How might you expand? (Did your initial test succeed? What might happen next as a result? Investigators constantly update their knowledge and refine their work based on the clues they find. Similarly, we need to avoid the temptation to conflate one successful test with The Truth in some absolute sense. Investigators never stop testing. They're lifelong learners. Are you?)

Now we've reached our final obstacle. Armed with six powerful questions to hone our intuition and think for ourselves, we have to turn inspiration and education into the only thing that matters: action. If we really want to escape the endless cycle of conventional thinking, we need to overcome the Final Boss. We're finally ready to drag him out from where he's hiding, strap him to a chair, turn the lamp on his face, and get to the bottom of this mystery.

* * *

INVESTIGATE YOUR CONTEXT

Ask the right questions to hone your intuition
and make the best decisions for your situation
(regardless of the best practice).

PIECE OF YOUR CONTEXT	TRIGGER QUESTION	CONFIRMATION QUESTION
You	What is your aspirational anchor?	What is your unfair advantage?
Your Audience	What is your first-principle insight?	Who are your true believers?
Your Resources	What are your constraints?	How might you expand?

CHAPTER 7

BREAK THE WHEEL

What if I told you that somebody thinks for themselves? What kind of person comes to mind?

Maybe a rebel. Johnny Cash fits that idea, dressed in black as he grips his guitar like a shotgun and stares apathetically off-camera. Cash marched to his own beat, regardless of what others thought.

Or maybe you picture a genius, like Albert Einstein, with his frizzy hair and chalkboard full of formulas.

Perhaps you hear a legendary voice instead, someone whose words reverberate deep within your bones. "People will forget what you said, people will forget what you did, but people will never forget how you made them feel." Maya Angelou certainly thought for herself.

Maybe, instead of a badass musician or brilliant physicist or uplifting poet, you imagine a weirdo full of quirks. They've got an unkempt look, with ragged clothing and paint-stained fingers. They'd never go work for The Man, oh no. Instead, they live in a loft apartment in a seedy area of town, muttering to a houseplant as they paint images of frogs on canvas, wood, and ceramic—yanno, *that* old career path.

Imagine a person who thinks for themselves. What do you see in your mind?

We have all these preconceived notions of what "thinking for yourself" looks like. You have to be a rebel, a genius, an inspiring voice, or some kind of quirky individual. It's as if we've *radicalized* the very idea of thinking for yourself. This is totally and completely broken. In your career, thinking for yourself isn't a radical thing to do. It's a *necessary* thing to do, if you want to do your best work.

We have to rethink what "thinking for yourself" means. If we don't, I fear this entire journey has been in vain. This book would become nothing more than a nice distraction from the daily grind—escapism, akin to science fiction. That would be perversely appropriate, too, since our desires to do exceptional work can sometimes feel like fantasy when we want to improve upon the status quo. We read stories of innovators and entrepreneurs and artists as if they're superheroes or mythical gods. Then there's us mortal humans, slogging through the suck. We could never, never reach those heights. We're down here in the real world doing what's practical.

Here's the deal: Thinking for yourself *is* practical. It's the most practical thing you can do, if only you'd spend half as much time investigating your context as you do searching for best practices. We need to change the narrative.

All the actions taken by the people we've met in these pages can be misconstrued as radical. If all we knew were the best practices of their industries, their work might seem unthinkable. However, once we heard their side of the story, it seemed quite logical, strategic, or even safe. The difference, of course, was context. We lacked context before hearing their tales.

At first, it seemed crazy for Mike Brown to roast robusta coffee beans—until we understood his aspiration. It was nuts for David Cancel to ask his team to remove lead forms from Drift's website—until we learned about his customers. Suzy Batiz had no business creating Poo-Pourri, and the bland, predictable Merriam-Webster Dictionary couldn't possibly become *this* widely loved. Paul Butler dancing around in a bird costume seems ridiculous, while Mikael Cho and Camille Ricketts faced high stakes and higher stress by doing something restrained or even small to build massive successes. It feels like the stuff of business lore...until you understand their side of the story.

These people aren't rebels, geniuses, legends, or weirdos, and any conclusion to the contrary can only be made in retrospect, when we put neat little bows on stories we tell. In reality, they are exactly like us. They're mere mortals who want to do their best work and struggle against commodity crap. It's just that they sought their answers within their context rather than clinging to best practices. They asked the right questions of their environments to act like investigators, not experts. They thought for themselves in the face of endless conventional thinking.

They broke the wheel.

Like us, these fine people aspired to be great. Unlike us, they articulated their aspirational anchors and identified their unfair advantages. Have you?

Like us, they grew their companies by winning new customers and serving existing fans better and better. Unlike us, they began their process with some first-principle insights before rallying their true believers. Will you?

Like us, despite grand aspirations, they had limited resources. They couldn't throw money or people at their problems. Unlike us, they identified each new set of constraints and expanded through a constant series of testing and learning. Can you?

Some people might assume that all the individuals we've met succeeded because they didn't know any better. I'd argue they did know better. They knew their context better than any expert or best practice ever could.

What if you did too?

THE PICNIC EXPERIMENT

Just because thinking for yourself is practical doesn't mean it's easy. Far from it. The moment you put down this book and return to your work, you'll be oh-so tempted by the endless cycle of conventional wisdom and trendy tactics. For all my criticisms of that wheel of average work, I have to admit, it's wonderfully convenient. Because once you question best practices, you step into the unknown. If you're going to think for yourself, you'll have to get comfortable being uncomfortable.

To understand what I mean, we need to meet a guy named Jim Mourey and learn about a concept called "cultural fluency."

Jim Mourey is an assistant professor of marketing at

DePaul University in Chicago and holds a PhD in marketing and psychology from the University of Michigan. He's spent his career studying how subtle cues influence our choices and behaviors. When we spoke, he recalled a pivotal moment in his career that, on the surface, seemed rather innocuous.

In his mid-twenties, as he was exploring the city of Paris, he noticed a woman take a cigarette out of her purse and start smoking. That seems simple enough, but Jim couldn't stop wondering: why do we constantly make mindless decisions?

"I'd grown up in a generation in the states where smoking is this horrible, abhorrent thing that nobody should do," Jim said. "Here was a woman who was non-consciously going through the motions and smoking a cigarette."

When something feels easy and familiar to us, why do we seem to abandon critical thinking, even if what we're doing isn't a good decision? It turns out the culprit is a phenomenon known as cultural fluency.

"In every culture, there are expectations of what's acceptable and what's not acceptable," Jim said. "If something is unfolding in a way that we'd predict it would, that would be an experience that's culturally fluent. And when something is fluent, we don't have to think very hard about it because the world is happening as it should."

On the other hand, when something seems unexpected or different or even counter to conventional norms, that experience is considered culturally "disfluent." Unfortunately for those who want to think critically for themselves, culture operates in the background. We don't often notice its effects but are influenced by them when we make decisions. Something that feels culturally fluent becomes more like an automatic behavior than a conscious choice, and that can be incredibly dangerous if our goal is to make the best possible decision in a given situation.

"Culture guides our behavior on a very subconscious level, so when things feel culturally fluent, we go with the flow, and when they feel culturally disfluent, we stop, hesitate, and think a little bit harder." This was Jim's hypothesis. To snap out of any pattern of mindless decision making, you can introduce some cultural disfluency.

Unfortunately, that might feel rather uncomfortable. Since moments of cultural fluency happen so organically that we hardly notice, moments that are culturally disfluent create some discomfort. In the workplace, that can feel nearly impossible to tolerate. Jim understood this, and he set out to test just how *much* disfluency a person needs to experience to make better decisions. Naturally, he decided to run a test at his mom's Fourth of July party, experimenting on unsuspecting friends and family. You know, typical picnic stuff.

As guests approached the buffet table full of hot dogs, hamburgers, and sides, Jim handed them plates. Half of the group received festive plates covered in American flags and fireworks, while the other half received plain white plates. Without knowing it, these guests had just been enlisted in a psychological test. Because picnic stuff.

Waiting at the end of the buffet, Jim then weighed each of their plates. The results revealed the unseen power of cultural fluency. "What we found was that people with the Fourth of July plates took significantly more food than the people who got the white plates."

Jim surmised that, since the Fourth is an American holiday based on gorging yourself, it felt natural to those guests with festive plates to take more food. Those with white plates, however, were disrupted ever so slightly and subconsciously from the mindless flow of the holiday enough to consider what they were doing.

Later that year, Jim ran the test again, experimenting once more on his friends and family, this time at a Labor Day picnic. In this iteration of the test, half the guests received white plates while the other half got plates intended for Halloween. As he predicted, people with the starkly out-of-place pumpkins and ghosts on their plates took less food than people with white plates.

"So taken together, we get at least initial support for this idea that, when there's a cultural fit, when things are as they should be, people don't really think. They tend to go with the flow. But when there's a disconnect, suddenly things are strange. They're not so strange that consciously we think, 'Oh, I should take less food.' It's just that, for automatic behaviors, we do them less. We hesitate a bit."

We hesitate a bit—that line really stood out to me. When our minds urge us to follow a best practice, what if we hesitated just a bit? That would create the necessary space we need to think more critically. According to Jim Mourey, when our minds notice a disconnect between what we expect and what actually happens, even if that disconnect is small, we tend to make more informed decisions. Those moments of cultural disfluency awaken our brains to the reality right in front of our faces that we'd otherwise miss as we follow the flow of familiar behavior. In that way, small moments that are uncomfortable can trigger the use of our intuition, i.e., that ability we have to contemplate our environment.

Now here's my question: What if we could *proactively* create moments of cultural disfluency? What if we could awaken our intuition on demand? By asking questions of the world around us, we can create some small but necessary distance between us and an expected behavior or flow. That helps us begin to form a more thoughtful answer. In other words, when we act like investigators, we break from cultural fluency to begin thinking more critically.

"There are people who subsist in the status quo," Jim said. "These are the people who see the numbers, they're meeting the numbers, and life is good, so they don't need to change anything. But if you want to be truly innovative, what my research suggests is that this is not the correct approach. If you truly want to innovate and change, you need to break up that flow. This can be something as crazy as redesigning the workspace so it creates an experience of disfluency, or it can be something as simple as traveling."

We don't need to make ourselves unbearably uncomfortable to think more critically about our work. Sure, overhauling your entire workspace could do the trick, but so could a quick trip to a new location, or maybe a plate that looks slightly out of place at the family picnic. Yes, quitting your job to try to build something entirely new and different removes you from the daily flow, but so does simply asking good questions to better understand and test things around you. We need only experience some slight discomfort, and suddenly, we're paying more attention. Our intuition has been activated. It can really be that simple and small. What matters is that we can see things more clearly, think for ourselves, and make the best decisions for us. We don't need to do anything radical to achieve that.

As we established earlier, intuition is the act of considering the world. Thanks to Jim Mourey, we've identified what appears to be the biggest barrier to doing so: cultural fluency. However, I actually think that cultural fluency is a symptom. It's not the illness. Yes, it prevents us from thinking for ourselves, but we aren't trying to merely *think* for ourselves. The entire purpose of this journey we've taken is to *act* in better ways. We want to create better work. That may start with making better decisions, but we're not making these decisions in our heads. They have to inform and change our work each day. So if cultural fluency is the symptom, the blocker to better thinking, then what's the illness? What is the final barrier between you and taking *action*?

You.

THE FINAL BARRIER

There's an old concept preached by Del Close, the late comedian considered by many to be the father of modern improv comedy. Close taught students like Tina Fey, Stephen Colbert, Dan Aykroyd, John Belushi, Chris Farley, Bill Murray, and Amy Poehler. He liked to tell his students, "Follow the fear."

When we encounter fear, the natural tendency is to avoid it, to retreat, and to resume our search for comfort. Once we experience anything disfluent, we prefer the safe confines of cultural fluency. Del Close may not have known the scientific terms, but he knew this behavior was a problem when improvising on stage. The gruff but hilarious comedian encouraged his students to identify those moments where they felt most uncomfortable during a performance and to explore them further. He wanted them to see where those paths could take them. That fear signaled some kind of new frontier, which would be rich with great material. Close believed that following the fear could yield his students' best work.

Thinking for yourself is a form of improvisation. One of my best friends, Kevin Mazzarella, is a Grammy-nominated music teacher who likes to tell his jazz students, "Improvisation is just composition in the moment." When we reason from first-principles and trust our intuition, we're composing our thoughts in the moment, in our specific context. We're far more similar to Close's or Mazzarella's students than we might realize. Just like them, we should follow the fear. And make no mistake, things will get scary.

Questioning conventional thinking is, after all, a lot harder than critiquing some expert you've never met. When we act like investigators, we also question our bosses, our clients, our peers—even ourselves and the things we assume we know.

It can feel impractical if not downright impossible to follow the fear in the workplace, not because of the "fear" part but because of the "follow" part. Again, this is about taking action. It's one thing to question a best practice in our minds. It's an entirely different matter to act on it. Thus, our final obstacle isn't the ability to break from cultural fluency to think for ourselves. Our goal isn't to merely hone our intuition, it's to trust it. The difference between average and exceptional work is the difference between *knowing* what we should do and actually *doing it.*

> **Thinking for yourself is a form of improvisation—composition in the moment.**

Few people understand this internal battle quite like Tim Urban, creator of the incredibly popular blog Wait But Why. (We met him briefly back in the fifth chapter.)

"I overcame myself," he told me when I asked what led to his success. "I won the battle against myself, which honestly, for a huge percentage of people who want to create their own career, the biggest battles are against themselves."

Tim's essays are notorious for their blend of humor, visual

metaphors (including plenty of stick figures and cartoon characters he invents), and deep but colloquial analyses on complex topics. To call his posts lengthy would be an understatement. They run thousands and sometimes tens of thousands of words apiece.

Wait But Why is a grab-bag of topics. In one early breakout hit, "Why Generation Y Yuppies Are Unhappy," Tim explored the damage done to the psyche of millennials thanks to both their expectations of adult life and their friends' carefully manicured portrayals of their own happiness on social media. Other topics include the Fermi Paradox (whether life exists in the universe); how to find a mate for life (featuring Tim's invention, the "Figured It All Out Staircase"); why we care what others think about us (explained by an adorable yet frustrating creature called the Social Survival Mammoth); and a four-part series about Elon Musk and the various industries his companies occupy. Tim wrote that series after a very unexpected phone call from one very impressed Wait But Why fan, Elon Musk himself.

So if Musk is, as Tim's first article calls him, "The World's Raddest Man," it's my opinion that Tim Urban is The World's Raddest Blogger. His millions of readers might agree. Tim's entertaining style and passionate fan base have led to a career in writing and speaking, including a 2016 TED Talk which has been viewed over 15 million times.

Whenever I see the name of Tim's blog, I can't help but think about the ideas we've explored together, and how important it is to stop and ask questions. That's how we escape the endless cycle of average work. When I first spoke with Tim, I asked if "Wait But Why" could also mean "Stop and Ask."

"Absolutely," he said. "That applies to creative work, but it also applies to the life path you're on. It applies to your routines and a bunch of things that a lot of people always say that on their deathbed they regret."

On your deathbed, you have clarity. You're unhooked from cultural fluency and conventional wisdom—whether because you possess your own wisdom or because, in your final moments, you no longer *care* about those things. Tim believes we should try to find that same level of deathbed clarity while there's still plenty of time in our lives left to care.

"I think a big goal in life should be to get that clarity earlier so you can actually do something about those things before they become regrets," he said. "You want to live your best life and live the life that makes sense for you."

Tim says that the longer you live, the more you begin to suspect that invisible forces out of your control shape your life—those same forces we learned about from Jim Mourey. Maybe, like Mike Brown before he launched Death Wish Coffee, you realize that your decision to get a graduate degree or to pursue accounting wasn't your decision so much as your family's expectations of what a great career looks like. Maybe, like the publishers of *The Independent* before they shrank their pages from broadsheets to tabloid size, you assume the traditional path is the one that works. But does any of "what works" in general apply to you specifically? Is the culturally fluent path actually the best path for you to take? These are the types of questions Tim believes we should ask more often.

"I think we'd all benefit from basically saying, 'Why do I think this actually? Why is the world like this?' Then you realize, the world is like this, or society believes this, because of something that happened in 1860 that doesn't apply anymore."

If we were to play that "why" game more often, Tim believes we'd realize that what we assume is the right decision for ourselves is actually the product of another person or trend influencing our behavior. "If you really think hard about it, you humble up and realize you're not sure what the best life is for you, and you have a lot of thinking and soul-searching to do," he said. "That feels really bad at the time, but it can save you from death-bed regrets."

Tim has heard a ton of people's regrets because of an article he wrote in 2013 called "Why Procrastinators Procrastinate." To this day, he continues to hear from readers about why their lack of action in life has created countless regrets. Of course, to explain why people struggle to break that inertia, Tim didn't use any technical phrases like "cultural fluency." Instead, he did something very Tim-like. He introduced the Instant Gratification Monkey.

According to the article, we all possess a Rational Decision-Maker who helms our brains. He (or she) wants to do things that make the most sense for us. (Arguably, it's the Rational Decision-Maker who wants to question best practices to ensure we do exactly that.) Unfortunately, living in our brains alongside this helpful fella is a rather unhelpful nuisance: the Instant Gratification Monkey. Unlike his roommate, the monkey "concerns himself entirely with maximizing the ease and pleasure of the current moment."

This monkey is the reason we don't stop and ask questions. He's the reason we prefer to do what feels mindless instead of saying, "Wait, but why?"

As Tim explained in his TED Talk, the Instant Gratification Monkey prevents us from thinking critically and making good choices. When the Rational Decision-Maker decides to do something productive, the monkey doesn't like that plan. "So he takes the wheel, and he says, 'Actually, let's read the entire Wikipedia page of the Nancy Kerrigan/Tonya Harding scandal because I just remembered that happened. Then we're gonna go over to the fridge, and we're gonna see if there's anything new in there since ten minutes ago. After that, we're gonna go on a YouTube spiral that starts with Richard Feynman talking about magnets and ends much, much later with us watching interviews with Justin Bieber's mom.'"

When Tim describes the monkey's obsession with doing

whatever feels easiest, he does so in the context of our home lives. For instance, if we're going for a run, the monkey wants us to stop, because not running is a lot easier than running. In addition to affecting us at home, however, I think that little nuisance has started following us into work. When we're presented with a problem, rather than try to figure it out, the monkey urges us to Google it or download a template or read a list of steps from someone else. The monkey sees an infinite and instantly accessible amount of cheats, hacks, shortcuts, and instructions, and he urges us to take that path instead of the harder one where we think for ourselves.

When Tim first introduced this devious little creature in his article, it was meant as a way to explain his own procrastination. Wait But Why's tagline used to be "New Post Every Week." Over time, Tim changed that to "Every Two Weeks." Today, the blog promises "New Posts Every Sometimes." Once Tim published the piece, however, it became something far bigger and more meaningful than a playful romp through his mind.

Tim quickly realized he'd stumbled onto a widespread problem that often paralyzes people whenever they think about doing anything better with their lives. The piece exploded in readership. It's been shared 480,000 times on social media. More than 450 people have left comments on the blog post—passionate outpourings of how the article made them feel. It seemed to Tim that everyone else also struggles to think longer term and make better, more thoughtful decisions.

The people who reached out to Tim weren't struggling to ship a single project or meet a deadline. In his words, "Long-term procrastination had made them feel like a spectator in their own lives. The frustration was not that they couldn't achieve their dreams—it's that they weren't even able to start chasing them."

From the outside looking in, it appears as though Tim is chasing his dream without much of a problem. He seems to be doing his best work. He writes about what he wants, when he wants. He makes money speaking and selling merchandise. He has a business partner and an assistant. He's an internet celebrity. Tim Urban seems like one of those guys who "made it." Of course, this is far from reality.

"I really don't enjoy the process," he said. In writing each article, he constantly faces that internal battle. With each twist and turn, he resists the urge to take shortcuts, and he also resists copying how other bloggers tend to write.

To start his process for a given article, Tim does hours upon hours of research. He likes that part, since he enjoys learning. But then things get hard.

"Then you have to be an architect, and all you have is a pile of metal and wood and nails. What's the design for the house? There's no right answer, which is kind of tortuous." It'd be far easier to package his research into a proven format like a list or slideshow, but Tim can't bear the thought of acting like everyone else. He wants to create something exceptional. He wants to be an exception. Then, suddenly, it happens: the post begins to make sense. Several big points connect in logical fashion, wrapped in the warm embrace of a funny metaphor or witty personal story. Tim breathes a sigh of relief. He loves life again. The Rational Decision-Maker has taken the controls. He's consumed by the work, mindful of every decision he's making.

Then he starts writing and hears a faint little chirping in his mind. "It's the dreaded blank screen with the blinking cursor that I used to hate in high school. I haven't written one word yet. It's this empty thing. So that's not fun."

Fun? Did someone say...fun? Out comes the monkey, and he starts whispering to the Rational Decision-Maker. *Psst. Hey. Just gimme the controls. Let's watch Game of Thrones. Wait, let's read some fan theories on Reddit! WAIT! Let's WATCH some fan theories on YouTube!*

"I'm back in misery," Tim said. But he muscles through another few paragraphs, and suddenly, he feels good again.

"But then I start drawing!" (Oh no.) "I'm a terrible artist." (Good grief.) "I'll draw a bench, and then I'll do like ten different benches and decide they all look ridiculous."

Then his hand will cramp, and he'll drop the pen and shake out his hand, then get back to drawing, then wrestle the monkey again, then finish his drawing, then the monkey squawks, then he edits his writing...and so on. It never ends.

"There are different kinds of misery. This is misery that somehow feels good. I'm doing hard work, and it's good work, important work." Tim knows the other type of misery that comes when all we do is ship commodity work, day in and day out. "I'll take this kind of misery over that misery any day. It's hard, but it's a little 'no pain, no gain.' If you want to get in shape, you have to go to the gym, and that's gonna hurt. But it's worth it."

Of course, in reality, there is no monkey whispering in our ears. There's also no Rational Decision-Maker. There's only us. All those characters are all us. That means what we choose to do or not do is entirely *on* us. We can't blame any metaphorical monkey. We have to win the battle within.

"Why did Wait But Why work?" Tim said to me. "Well, because this guy won a couple big battles against himself."

How can we do that too? Tim has an idea. In his article, he introduces a third character living in our brains, one capable of defeating the Instant Gratification Monkey. This new guy is called the Panic Monster. He's our guardian angel since he's the one thing that can scare off the monkey. The Panic Monster is essentially an extreme version of cultural disfluency. For procrastinators, he wakes up when a deadline approaches, chasing away the monkey so they can actually do some work. The monster snaps us out of our mindless lulls.

I also think he makes for an excellent partner to a well-honed intuition. If we merely panicked, we might make poor decisions all over again. But if we know our aspirational anchor, have a first-principle insight, and understand our resource constraints, and we're still afraid to act...perhaps we need a little more urgency to follow the fear. Sure, we may not have a deadline on our calendars for everything we do at work, but everything we do has a deadline. Eventually, our entire careers have a deadline, and really, so do we. If that doesn't spur action, I don't know what will.

> "The frustration was not that they couldn't achieve their dreams—it's that they weren't even able to start chasing them."
> —Wait But Why creator/author Tim Urban

In the end, the only way to do exceptional work is to *act* on the information that makes our situation an exception. If we merely start and stop our thinking with a best practice, we're missing crucial context when we make decisions. Thus, for something to truly be the "best" for us, we have to *contextualize* it to our situation. It shouldn't matter if we use all, some, or none of a popular convention or even our own ideas. We shouldn't care if what we're doing feels old, new, or somewhere in between. In our quest to do our best work, the only thing that matters is that we figure out what works best *for us*.

Throughout this book, we've met some people whose stories have inspired you. We've distilled those stories into some questions we can ask. Now we need to go and answer them, each in our own situations. We need to think for ourselves and, most crucially, turn that intuition into action. And lest you begin to question your ability to do so, I have one final story to tell.

SALLY'S APIZZA

New Haven's Little Italy is a rather literal interpretation of its name. First of all, it's extremely little. (Wooster Street runs just 0.3 miles.) It's also extremely Italian. Short but feisty *nonni* watch groups of *bambini* as they play in one of the two parks on the side of the one-way street. Leather-skinned men with balding, round heads and even rounder bellies sit in lawn chairs on the sidewalk in front of several unmarked concrete buildings. (I'm told they're "men's clubs," and I will ask no more questions.) The street is splashed with red, white, and green as Italian flags fly over the men's clubs and banners hang off streetlights and over doorways, each leading into a new paradise of pasta, pastry, or pizza. It's the latter that draws crowds to Wooster Street each night.

This extremely little, extremely Italian street in Connecticut punches above its weight class when it comes to pizza. Each year, according to publications like *USA Today*, the Daily Meal, Thrillist, and Eater, New Haven ranks at or near the top of the list for pizza cities, largely thanks to the two heavyweights that make up one of the culinary world's fiercest rivalries: Sally's and Pepe's.

Officially known as Sally's Apizza and Frank Pepe Pizzeria Napoletana, the two share a street and a bloodline. Italian immigrant Frank Pepe created the original joint on Wooster Street in 1925, while his nephew, Salvatore Consiglio, a.k.a. Sally, decided to strike out on his own in 1938. He set up shop just one block away. The two places have been at odds ever since.

I grew up just two towns east of New Haven, so I'm intimately familiar with this rivalry. I also grew up in an Italian family, so I'm utterly obsessed with Wooster

Street pizza. However, if you're a true believer in New Haven pizza, you have to choose your place of worship. For as long as I can remember, my family has been going to Sally's. It's my favorite pizza in the world, and it will be my children's favorite, and my children's children's, and my children's children's children's. (For those few readers who know New Haven pizza, a quick aside: if you're thinking, "I dunno, Bar or Modern might be the best pizza," I invite you to gently rest this book upon the table, arise from your chosen perch, and take a long walk off a short pier.)

As I was saying: Sally's. End of debate.

Unfortunately, despite my religion on the matter, I nearly committed a mortal sin as a child. It all started when Lorenzo, our usual waiter, dropped by to take our order. Lorenzo attended Yale, where he was an accomplished swimmer. After graduating, he chose to work at Sally's. (Because he wanted to work in heaven, that's why.)

I'd guess Lorenzo is six-foot-five. He towered over his customers as he sauntered around the tiny, red-tiled room that is Sally's. Regardless of the weather, he wore khaki shorts, exposing his alarmingly muscular calves. With a wry smile, he both welcomed his regulars and teased newcomers about not knowing the rules. (They serve pizza. Nothing more. Beer. Never wine.) One time, partway through the typical hour-long wait for our pizza, Lorenzo brought a pair of dice to our table and showed my family a game he used to play for a few bucks with old friends. Did he have tables to fill and orders to take? Undoubtedly. Did he seem to care? Lorenzo's not a guy who seems to have a care in the world.

"Pizza's coming right out," he said, leaving us to our dice game. It took forty-five additional minutes. (Worth it.)

When I was a kid, I asked Lorenzo a pretty dangerous question. I knew that Pepe's was just down the street and that they, too, made pizza—a simple dish with just a few ingredients. "So," I wondered, "what makes Sally's any different?"

"Well, let's see" said Lorenzo, who could have removed my smug grin with a swift kick from one of those calves. "We both have access to the same sauce. We both have access to the same cheese, and we both have access to the same toppings. But the secret is the starter."

The starter is a simple mixture of yeast and water, and it forms the basis for making dough. There are two ways to affect your starter once you create the original mixture: expose it to various things, and let it sit over time. You can expose your starter to different levels of light and heat and air or even squeeze a few drops from a handful of grapes into the mix. As the mixture begins to bubble, you can also feed the yeast with some flour and more water. Then, you can let it sit over time before using it to create your dough, combining a little scoop of the stuff with the rest of your ingredients.

Starters are vitally important for making great dough. In fact, some bakeries have been cultivating their starters for decades, as is the case with Sally's. Some starters are so important to the process that bakers even give their starter a name, like it's a pet that lives in their home. (I don't have a starter, but if I did, I know exactly what I'd call mine: the Yeastie Boys. Let's just move on.)

In the end, thanks to the various ways the starter has been affected, no two starters make the same dough. That's how Sally's can make amazing pizza that's somehow different than their competitor down the street. That's how they can use the same exact cheese and toppings and even sauce, and still end up with pies that taste vastly different. The most important part of their process is the starter.

So what does this have to do with our attempt to do exceptional work? Well, given all the things that you've been exposed to throughout your life—every experience, hobby, hope, and fear—I think that *you* are the starter in your work. Whether or not a large corporation or an "influencer" with a platform likes to admit this, every situation is unique. There's no repeatable process that doesn't need updating, and no final seven-step guide to guarantee results. And it's all thanks to you. You are the biggest variable and least predictable part of your context.

Just as important as any list of tips and tricks from an industry expert is the fact that, say, you grew up in Saratoga Springs, New York, and you hated being an accountant, but you love lounging around coffee shops, and you aspire to create the world's strongest coffee. Just as critical as the latest and greatest trends and technologies is your realization that, yanno, you're a pretty charming communicator, just as comfortable talking to poor families on a tropical island as you are to Congress. You have no scruples in the way you act, which means that dancing around in a giant parrot costume might just be the best decision...for you.

Maybe you're a driven marketer trying to create a documentary film. Maybe you're a big brand executive with an English literature degree, or an entrepreneur with an eye for great photographs, or an author who grew up eating some damn good pizza in New Haven. Whatever the case, whomever you are, *you* are the starter.

And no two starters make the same dough.

In this era flooded with conventional thinking, it has

never been easier to be average. I say, let's be something else: the exception. Exceptional work happens when we find and follow what makes us an exception. So what makes *you* an exception?

Start your investigation by asking the right questions of your context.

First, develop your sense of self-awareness, whether alone or with your team. Ask the right questions about that first, all-important piece of your context: you.

PIECE OF YOUR CONTEXT	TRIGGER QUESTION	CONFIRMATION QUESTION
You The person or people doing the work.	**What is your aspirational anchor?** Your intent for the future, combined with some hunger you have today, some dissatisfaction. Turn your vague desire to do exceptional work into something specific and concrete. Give yourself the first filter, through which you can vet best practices as possibilities—they serve you, not the other way around.	**What is your unfair advantage?** What is it about you or your team that uniquely qualifies you to reach that aspiration? Make no mistake: You are the one thing your competitors can't access. You are the starter, the unfair advantage. Are you using that fully in your work?

Next, develop your sense of situational awareness. No part of your situation is more vital to your success than your specific audience—whether that means your customers, prospects, readers, viewers, listeners, or even a boss or client you're trying to help or persuade. For whom are you creating your work? Ask the right questions about them.

PIECE OF YOUR CONTEXT	TRIGGER QUESTION	CONFIRMATION QUESTION
You	**What is your aspirational anchor?**	**What is your unfair advantage?**
Your Audience The person or people receiving the work.	**What is your first-principle insight?** A foundational but hard-to-reach truth. If you can reach it, you can build back up more original thinking from there, making better decisions because you started in a better place. Your work might end up looking crazy to others, but your insight makes that creative, innovative approach seem logical, because you truly understand your audience's situation.	**Who are your true believers?** A small number of people who react in big ways to what you're doing. Addressing the first-principle insight about your audience's situation creates an emotional response. Have you done so? If not, revisit your insight. Otherwise, use that reaction as a signal of success: focus your work in that direction, even if it breaks from the best practice.

Finally, you need to make the work happen, and in doing so, you must understand your resources. Your goals, metrics, budget, headcount, timeline, and more—they all create a set of limitations, a sort of box within which you might actually be more creative. To do so, however, you need to understand the walls of that box. Ask yourself the right questions about your resources.

PIECE OF YOUR CONTEXT	TRIGGER QUESTION	CONFIRMATION QUESTION
You	What is your aspirational anchor?	What is your unfair advantage?
Your Audience	What is your first-principle insight?	Who are your true believers?
Your Resources The means to make the work happen.	What are your constraints? Creative freedom doesn't work. It may not even exist. But that's okay, since we'll come up with more ideas *and* better ideas once we understand our guardrails and goalposts. We can test our thinking in focused ways after answering previous questions above. Our goal will be learning quickly so we can scale our work based on results, not precedents or trends. After all, that's ultimately what matters most: results, whether we measure in data or personal fulfillment.	How might you expand? Not from one constrained box to the wide-open field, but from one box to another in an ongoing process of testing and learning. It's far better to be vaguely right than precisely wrong, since each situation changes far too much to cling to any one convention or trend. Become a lifelong learner who constantly improves, an investigator who obsesses over asking questions, finding evidence, and updating your knowledge.

This is your "instant clarity generator"—your intuition made concrete and useful. This is how to investigate your context, and this is the information that best practices miss.

When we ask good trigger questions, we spark our curiosity and begin our investigation. We put a little distance between us and that ever-spinning wheel, creating some necessary cultural disfluency to begin thinking for ourselves.

When we ask good confirmation questions, we ensure we're on the right path toward our goals when we take action. That's the entire point: turning better thinking into better action.

PIECE OF YOUR CONTEXT	TRIGGER QUESTION	CONFIRMATION QUESTION
You	What is your aspirational anchor?	What is your unfair advantage?
Your Audience	What is your first-principle insight?	Who are your true believers?
Your Resources	What are your constraints?	How might you expand?

These are the six questions I've identified along this journey with you. However, I wouldn't be listening to my own message if I didn't encourage you to find your own too. If these questions work for you, that's great. If you substitute others or identify more, then that's even better. (By the way, share them with me any time—I'm hyper-responsive on social media or reachable via email at jay@unthinkablemedia.com.) What matters isn't that we stick to anyone's framework, including mine. What matters is that we ask questions, foregoing the notion that anyone else has "the" answers for us. What matters is that we understand how to find our own, changing what we know as our context changes.

I'm not asking you to do anything radical. I'm not asking you to be a rebel, a genius, a legend, or a weirdo. I'm not asking you to follow anyone else's definition of what it means to be exceptional. I'm asking you to find your own. I'm asking you to think for yourself in this world overflowing with conventional thinking.

This book is your sledgehammer. You've stared at it for a while now. You've curled your fingers around it, grasping it tight, lifting it to your side. But in the end, it's utterly useless...unless you're willing to start swinging.

Today, you face a choice. I know you'd tell me that you *don't* aspire to do average work, but now, I'm asking you to prove it. If you want to be average, follow the best practice. If you truly want to be exceptional, craft your own. Pick up that sledgehammer, and just keep swinging it. In every new situation you encounter, with every new detail that changes your context, just keep asking questions and investigating. Just keep swinging away. Your best work won't be created by the answers others give you, but by the questions you ask yourself. So starting today, right now, do what others might consider unthinkable—not because you're doing anything radical, but because in a world full of so much average work, you know what it takes to do something exceptional.

Go break the wheel.

ABOUT THE AUTHOR

JAY ACUNZO has served as a digital media strategist at Google and held multiple leadership positions at high-growth technology companies, including HubSpot. He spent three years as VP of Brand for the venture capital firm NextView before founding Unthinkable Media, which creates original series with B2B brands. He's been named to Boston's "50 on Fire" list and has been cited in the New York Times, The Washington Post, FastCompany, Fortune, Entrepreneur, and more. Jay currently writes the weekly newsletter "Damn the Best Practices," hosts his narrative-style podcast Unthinkable, and travels the world as a keynote speaker.

Made in the USA
Las Vegas, NV
13 May 2021